PAST LIVES

PAST LIVES

Dilys Gater

Chivers Press • Thorndike Press
Bath, England   Thorndike, Maine USA

This Large Print edition is published by Chivers Press, England and by Thorndike Press, USA.

Published in 1998 in the U.K. by arrangement with Robert Hale Ltd.

Published in 1998 in the U.S. by arrangement with Robert Hale Ltd.

U.K. Hardcover ISBN 0-7540-3169-1   (Chivers Large Print)
U.S. Softcover   ISBN 0-7862-1287-X (General Series Edition)

The text of this Large Print edition is unabridged.
Other aspects of the book may vary from the original edition.

Set in 16 pt. New Times Roman.

Printed in Great Britain on acid-free paper.

British Library Cataloguing in Publication Data available

Library of Congress Catalog Card Number: 97-91168

ISBN: 0–7862–1287–X (lg. print : sc)

To all those
who have shared their past lives with me so
generously,
and especially to Richard

I shall light a candle of understanding in thine
heart: which shall not be put out
2 Esdras 14:25

The dogs bark, but the caravan passes on
Eastern proverb

CONTENTS

CONTENTS

Author's Note

I am a practising psychic, medium and healer. In the course of my work, I deal for much of the time with the spiritual, rather than the physical and material, state of the person consulting me, and this often involves examining that person's past—including their past lives, or previous existence.

The case histories detailed in this book are genuine ones; where possible they have been checked with the person concerned and included with their full approval. Any small details that might have been reported inaccurately are the result of my memory reaching back over hundreds of past-life sittings. These have been conducted over a long period of time and often in the most unlikely places: the Wedding and Evening Gown Department of a luxurious dress shop, for instance, or on the telephone to people in all parts of the country whom I have never met, or in a working jeweller's room at the back of the shop, where I met a very royal lady.

All names have been changed to safeguard privacy. A few cases involved myself, and these and any interviews conducted have been incorporated into the third person and the overall style of the book.

Without the co-operation and goodwill of

the people included in this book, it could not exist. Theory in this case is like the bare bones, and just as dead. The problems, fears, triumphs, anxieties, loyalties and general human qualities of my sitters—not to mention the shining spiritual light they have provided to show me the way—are beyond thanks. But thank you anyhow.

Dilys Gater, London, 1997

PAST LIVES

CHAPTER ONE

I HAVE BEEN HERE BEFORE

I had been giving a talk on 'Past Lives: The Theory of Reincarnation' at a Psychic Fair. As I was returning to my table, a woman with soft, dark hair stopped me. She was holding a young boy by the hand, and two girls (obviously his sisters by the family resemblance) hovered behind them.

'I wonder,' she began. Then, looking down at the boy, 'It's just that ... Well. Jason can remember living in another life, before he was born. He has remembered it ever since he was about two, and he started talking to us about an airship—you know, those big, balloony things filled with gas. He said he remembered being on one when it caught fire.'

'Round the beginning of this century. That's fascinating,' I replied encouragingly.

'Would you ... I mean, could you find out more about it? Can you tell us anything further?'

I asked Jason's age, and, when told he was eight, I hesitated.

'Normally it isn't wise to attempt a formal sitting with a child,' I said to his mother. 'The patterns of present and future are not yet clear, and the high spiritual aspects that might emerge from this sort of work could seem frightening or upsetting.'

I turned to Jason.

'How do you feel about this? Does it bother you? Would you like to talk to me about your memories, or would you rather not?'

He was amazingly self-possessed and seemed much more mature than a child of eight.

'I don't mind,' he said disarmingly.

He had already, it seemed, discussed the subject with other people as well as his family, so I suggested an informal consultation with the boy and his mother only, the rest of the family removing themselves. Too many people can interfere with the vibrations and patterns of clairvoyant communication. (It is often possible, for instance, to lay out cards for a sitter and find that you have instead laid them out for a friend or companion who may be sitting alongside—or may not even be present physically.)

Jason's mother filled in the background for me. He had begun to talk about being on board the airship almost as soon as he had the words to communicate, and he had identified a picture of an airship at a very early age.

'We took him to people who understood that sort of thing—a professor, and psychic investigators—and they made notes and took it all down,' she said.

It appeared to me that the family neither questioned nor disbelieved Jason's story, and had never doubted that his recollections were

2

genuine. As his mother pointed out:

'He had never seen or heard of an airship, yet he knew what it was and what it was called, even at two.'

The obvious conclusion to be drawn was that Jason had, in some previous life in the early part of the century, been on an airship that had caught fire, and that he retained a memory of the incident which was just as valid as his memory of, say, whatever had happened to him within the last week.

* * *

Many people have reason to believe they may have 'been here before'. Apart from the question of whether we live lives other than the one we are living at the moment, there are literally hundreds of thousands of ordinary people who have experienced *déjà vu*—a sense of entering a place, scene or incident that they seem to know well and could describe in intimate detail, though they have never experienced it or had any knowledge of it before. Just as common is the feeling, when meeting certain people for the first time, that one knows them intimately and has known them always. 'We were close in some other life,' such people tell each other.

There are theories, which we will examine later, to explain how such aberrations can take place without necessarily signifying anything of

3

a psychic nature, but these do not convince people who have experienced the vivid realities. Past-life recall, flashes of memory or other personal experiences need no documentation or formal 'proof' to persuade those who choose to believe in them that time as we know it can allow us to go back (sometimes forwards) to existences that have already taken place or will happen in the future ... or that may be running alongside our own present time—like two tracks on a tape playing simultaneously.

Many times, in my work as a psychic, sitters have come to me and asked me to investigate their past lives, because they feel a strong affinity with a particular place or period of history. Some even tell me, for example, that, 'I know I was burned/drowned/persecuted as a witch'. It is surprising how many 'witches' one does encounter, and this is probably because in less enlightened centuries sensitive, psychic souls with seemingly supernatural powers were such a threat to 'ordinary' folk, as well as to authority that they were victimized almost as a matter of routine. The average person is fearful and intolerant of what he cannot understand.

Often the memory which survives of a past existence is of a traumatic episode (especially a traumatic death), and people who have far-back recollections of being 'drowned/burned/persecuted as a witch' are generally still sensitive, still possess psychic

4

awareness, and are still trying to follow their spiritual path in the best way they can.

It is easy enough for an enthusiastic convert to the concept of past lives to want to remember something, and often, unless one is very experienced, it may be difficult to differentiate between a genuine past-life recall and what could best be described as wishful thinking. Often, the veracity of the memory—for which one gets a 'feel' as one progresses—lies in the apparent ordinariness of what is recalled, the comparatively boring and meaningless triviality of it.

* * *

Francesca, young and dark, told me she knew she had lived as a Tudor woman.

'I have always known. I don't know who I was, just an ordinary person, but I have a vivid memory of leaning out of a window, watching the King's procession pass by. King Henry VIII. I can remember the little houses, the dress I was wearing, and waving as the procession passed.'

* * *

The theory of reincarnation, which teaches that the soul may be reborn through several (possibly many) lifetimes, is not just a sensational scam dreamed up by the tabloids and the mentally afflicted. It is commonly believed, for instance, that nearly everyone who regresses to a past life, or claims to have lived before, will automatically discover they 'were' Nefertiti or Alexander the Great, Marie Antoinette or Napoleon. In fact this is most unlikely, since there were far more common people about than kings, queens and historical figures. I am always extremely sceptical if I link up with a famous personage, and in the many hundreds of readings I have conducted into past lives, I have so far only experienced a handful that might have been of 'famous' historical men or women.

The theory of reincarnation forms an integral part of most recognized religions. Even Christianity speaks of 'life after death' and recognizes that the divine spark within each living creature will progress, in whatever way, beyond this current incarnation. In Buddhism, the progression of the divine spark, the soul, carries it through many lifetimes, from ignorance to high spiritual enlightenment, each life part of the learning process.

* * *

I was particularly interested in Jason's case, since I had never come across a past-life recollection in one so young. Being careful not to frighten him or to place ideas in his head, I questioned him about his memory of the airship.

6

'Can you tell me in your own words what you remember, Jason?'

'I was on the airship, and it crashed and there was a lot of fire everywhere.'

'What were you doing?'

'Standing up, just watching.'

'Sure? Not sitting?'

'No.' He shook his head. 'I was standing, watching.'

'What could you see?'

'People screaming, trying to get away. And the flames burning.'

'And where was the airship? What was it doing?'

He had difficulty in sorting this out, and I did not want to prompt him. Eventually I got the picture—the airship had been in the air, burning; it had not yet crashed. I was particularly careful to clarify this, but I deduced from what he told me that the airship must have been on the point of crashing, since it could not have lasted long in the air if it had been burning so fiercely.

I had by this time linked up with Jason's persona in his past life and asked him if he could tell me anything about who he remembered being—but without giving away any of my own thoughts.

'Were you yourself, like you are now? The same age?'

He found this difficult to answer.

'What were you wearing? Can you

7

remember?'

'Black shoes,' came after a moment.

I knew he had been wearing black shoes. I had seen them: shiny patent, the sort of shoes that a young man who was good at dancing would have worn in the early days of this century. He had been a young man in his late teens, a privileged person and a socialite.

I had by this time also seen something else, which I confided to his mother. He had been killed in the fire, and in fact the memory he retained had happened after his death. The body of that young man had fallen from the burning airship and was lying somewhere on the ground below. It did not seem to me possible that anyone who had been alive on the burning ship would have simply stood by quietly and watched the tragedy, making no move to help either himself or others, yet I had Jason's word for it and I was aware myself that it had been so. But he had been detached because it was not his physical body that was standing there; it was his spirit, which had by now left his body and was simply a helpless observer of the inferno.

* * *

Reincarnation and past lives must be taken on trust, there is no other way. Indeed, any effort to explain or justify their importance and relevance in a material sense, is likely to lead to

8

a no-win situation. If the 'life' or memory is vague and seemingly lacking in point or meaning—as many appear to be, until one begins to work on them—a sceptic will scoff that, 'It means nothing at all. Anyone could just make up something like that.' On the other hand, if the past lives that emerge are vitally linked with the sitter and his or her problems, the comment of worldly-wise cynics is that they are far too conveniently coincidental to be believed.

* * *

Take the case of Olwen, a woman in her fifties. It would be difficult for even the most imaginative fiction-writer to think up such a perfect scenario. But you have my word it happened just as I described it—and the real woman who is 'Olwen' is only one of many who will willingly testify to the difference their experience of a 'past-life sitting' has made to their attitude towards their present life.

Olwen consulted me initially because she had been trying all her life to learn to swim, with no success. Even when she began to make progress, the confidence somehow disappeared, and she returned, it seemed, to square one every time.

My feeling was that her inability to swim was in fact a symptom rather than the real problem. I saw that she had never felt in control of her life, or that she had any right to choose her own path—everything in the past having revolved around pleasing other people. She agreed that this made sense, though she had never considered her life in that light before. She also revealed that she felt guilty a lot of the time, though in fact, she had nothing with which to reproach herself. But lack of self-respect or of a sense of one's own worth is often linked to feelings of guilt, so I did not lay too much importance on this to begin with.

I told Olwen that the family jokes about her inability to learn to swim reflected the one choice she had actually made for herself. We all choose our roles, whether consciously or not, and she had—however unconsciously—decided at some stage that she *would not* swim. To the rest of the family it seemed like failure, but in fact it was Olwen's reinforcement of her identity and her right to choose.

She accepted this as a part of the personality difficulties we had discussed, and spoke at some length about ways in which she could gain strength and control to go forward with confidence and peace of mind. Her sitting was brought to a rather abrupt end (it was done on the phone—I was in London while she was in the Midlands), but just before it ended, she asked me whether it was possible that she had drowned in a previous life.

'From what I see of your personality, I think you would have been more likely to have been imprisoned, confined or restrained in some way, rather than drowned,' I told her, 'but I will link up to get a past life and see what comes.'

The pictures began to come through very quickly. I asked her whether she had ever visited the seaside as a child, and had an accident on the pier—I could see a large, old-fashioned pier seemingly miles high as it rose from the sand beneath.

'No, not to my knowledge,' she replied.

I told her that I thought she had fallen from a pier as a very young baby, and died, and we were then obliged to conclude the reading.

Afterwards, though, the vision continued to clarify itself, as it often does when I am dealing with past lives. Sometimes it emerges immediately, complete, as though I see a picture in which every detail is there. At other times I may have a cloudy vision that takes a little time to settle and can even change in emphasis and fact; what seemed to be a feminine personality may turn out to be masculine, or the members of a family or components of a scene may alter.

I knew a baby had fallen from a very high pier—much higher, in the view I had in my mind, than any ordinary pier would have been. I also saw a vision of a perambulator with white linen pillows and frills, moving violently up and down, empty. I knew clairvoyantly that someone had, in a fury of jealousy, jounced the baby carriage so that the baby had fallen from

11

it. At first I thought it had been a nanny or nursemaid, then the picture steadied. It had been a small girl of about five, who had vented her jealousy of her tiny baby brother by shaking his pram when their nurse or nanny had left them for a moment on the pier.

Olwen had not drowned in a past life—she had inadvertently caused her baby brother to drown. And that was why the vision of the pier which I had seen had been hugely magnified; I had seen it through the eyes of a small, very unhappy child, who all her life would carry the uneasy knowledge that—though she had been far too young to murder wilfully—she had been responsible for her brother's 'accident' and death in the water below.

Olwen listened in silence when I was able to tell her of what I had seen.

'I have never liked piers,' she said, 'I don't like the sea. Yes, it explains a lot.'

And the sense of a life 'imprisoned' in guilt—the small Victorian/Edwardian girl who had to live with what she had done and could not forgive herself—that made sense too.

* * *

Sitters do not always regress to a past life themselves and experience the emotions they felt in the past or feel that 'they were there'. Sometimes, as with Jason, this can happen spontaneously. Other people may regress under guidance from an experienced psychic or hypnotherapist. But most of the cases I have dealt with have meant that I link up with the past lives and then describe to the sitter what I have 'seen'.

Obviously it would be all too easy to 'con' the unsuspecting with fake descriptions like: 'You were Queen Elizabeth I', or 'You were one of the people on the *Titanic*'. As I have pointed out, it is next to impossible to prove the existence of a past life, even when the sitter provides details while regressed. Equally, most people would regard the prospect of being Queen Elizabeth I or a passenger on the *Titanic* with mild interest, but no more than that, and they would probably feel no emotion or sense of identification.

The 'feel' that marks a genuine past life comes not from remembering whether one was a man or a woman, and lived in medieval times or in the days of Queen Victoria, but from the deep sense of significance and meaning that the revelation can bring to life as we are living it today. Awareness of past lives often provides answers we may have been seeking for years, or helps to clarify emotions, inexplicable feelings or half-sensed unease. Often sitters will identify completely with the figures in their past lives, even though they do not actually remember the life itself and the situation may seem far removed from their position today. They may also feel that the individual they

13

were in the past is recognizable as some meaningful but lost fragment of their present personality.

Just as 'hunches' and 'gut feeling' may very well turn out to be a form of clairvoyant intuition, so emotional states can have a great deal to do with past lives. Many people express deep concern with the cause and effect of their past existence.

'I seem to be suffering so much in this life,' people ask, 'What did I do to deserve it?'

But often the answer is not as simple as that. In fact it is rarely simple at all, and anyone who can sum up a past-life situation in one sentence that explains everything is probably only skimming the surface—or simply telling the sitter what he or she wants to hear.

* * *

Justine did not ask 'What have I done?'; instead she told me:

'I know I have done something very wrong— probably committed a terrible crime.'

She was highly psychic and aware of a feeling of immense guilt that had haunted her all her life.

'I have been to a lot of psychics and tried to find the answer,' she said. 'But although I have been told all sorts of things, I still don't feel I have the solution.'

I never promise anything when undertaking

14

a past-life session, but in fact the powers that reveal these matters have rarely failed me. It is not my doing but the spiritual intelligence I am permitted to pass on to the sitter, and, except for occasions when it is obvious that the person concerned is hostile or actively antagonistic, there is always a vision of something to work on—even the odd times when I have been unable to link in with a 'life' have had significance in that person's development.

I went slowly into a past life for Justine. I got a picture of a dark, large and hellish interior, which I thought was of some kind of Victorian factory—dyeing cloth or something similar. There seemed to be no light, and the air was thick and clogged with fumes. I saw an enormous vat of a liquid that I knew instinctively was dangerous, like sulphur, or some other type of acid. Figures moved about: the workers.

'You didn't own this place,' I told Justine. 'I think you were related to the man who owned it. You took it on your soul, though—the deaths and sickness that happened there. Even though you could do nothing about it.'

She was thinking aloud.

'My husband has a factory—not like that, but I can't bear to go into the building. And the fumes . . . I get chest problems for no reason.'

Most sitters begin to make excited comparisons at an early stage in the session, and, though interesting, these are often

15

superficial compared to the real meaning of the 'life'. I said nothing but continued with the process of linking up again to the past.

It became obvious from the glimpses we received that Justine had been close to many situations where some form of injustice or cruelty took place, but she did not seem to have committed any act herself to account for the extreme personal guilt she felt. I proceeded with some difficulty, and was about to close the session—out of sheer tiredness (connecting with the past can be very tiring)—when a new image came clearly into my mind.

I saw a line of men—priests or holy men, I thought—walking through a narrow, rocky defile, and then there was a vision of some sort of underground cave, a powerful flood bursting into it, the rock collapsing, the men drowned and covered with the fallen roof within minutes. A crime on a very large scale—made even more terrible because whoever had ordered these executions had been responsible for the deaths of the innocent representatives of an entire religion.

I told Justine what I had seen and added: 'I thought they were Christian priests at first, but it was much earlier than that. I get the ruthlessness and self-willed power here of a Jezebel. I can't say you *were* Jezebel, but you were certainly someone very similar to her. Trying to wipe out the holy priests of a religion she would not allow. Completely cold, thinking only of herself, her own wants, her own way. Very sure of herself physically and mentally.'

We spoke for some time about this last 'life'. Justine was thrilled and declared that now she knew why she had felt guilty. That really had been on a grand scale. And Jezebel! I talked to her about the significance of past errors and the ways in which she might use them to guide her spiritual progress in this life. When we parted she said she felt it had been the most marvellous session, and that at last she could see the patterns of her existence falling into place.

But my private view about the importance of the session was not that it had come up with a neat answer to the question of why she felt guilty. The feeling of guilt was only, as with Olwen's swimming problem, a symptom. I could not tell Justine, but I could see that the manipulative nature that had sent the holy men to their deaths and that had somehow found itself involved in the exploitation of others in the Victorian factory was still very much a part of her personality. She herself was convinced that she had conquered her spiritual pride and was now in a position of genuine humility. In fact, my impression—which I knew she would not have taken kindly, even if I had tried to force it on her—was that she was basically no further forward in that respect than the lovely barbaric princess who had sent the holy men to their deaths.

*   *   *

Over and over again, past lives shed light on situations, and often in the most unexpected way. Dana had been raped over a long period as a child, and she had never tried to fight back, but had remained passive and withdrawn into herself. When, under light hypnosis, she regressed to a former life, she found herself the victim of another rapist: a brutal medieval soldier. She became extremely distressed, but when she was brought back to the present, she said eagerly:

'It was a painful experience, yes, but it has given me something so positive. That time, in that other life, I wasn't just a young girl being raped. I was a person who had been violated and who was able to express her outrage and anger. I really felt that I would kill him . . . that I had the strength to get an axe or dagger and hit out with all my might. I have never been able to feel anything about what happened in this life except guilt and shame, even though I know theoretically that it was not my fault—but it was wonderful to feel angry, to feel I had a right to defend myself . . . that I had a right *not* to be raped. I have never been able to feel it before, but I won't forget it.'

*   *   *

The more work one does on the subject of 'past lives', the more it becomes apparent that the

18

veil between what we call the past and what we recognize as the present is frail indeed. What we are in this life has a great deal to do with what we have been, and, in seemingly incredible fashion, the past can help to heal and guide us as we go forward to the future. Reincarnation is not just a sort of parlour game; past-life sessions and awareness can create whole new foundations of thought and belief, and can even—as I have witnessed many times in my work—help to perform seeming miracles.

CHAPTER TWO

MAKING CONTACT WITH THE PAST

The theory that we may have lived lives before our present ones is as old as humanity itself, but the concept of linking up in any way to these lives, is completely alien to most people in the western world. If not scornfully rejected as 'mumbo-jumbo', it is deeply and disturbingly shrouded in mystery and confusion.

In past centuries belief in reincarnation—commonly accepted in the East—was allowed by the early Christian Church to form a part of its own official teachings, until controversy within its ranks resulted in the synod, convened by the Emperor Justinian in 543 AD at

Constantinople, that condemned such beliefs. Later laws outlining just what the Emperor thought about previous lives included the following ominous warning:

'If anyone assert the fabulous pre-existence of souls, and shall assert the monstrous restoration which follows from it: let him be anathema.'

Under this threat of excommunication the pious abandoned the whole subject, so that it disappeared and went deeply 'underground'. Details were not available to the ordinary person, and those who attempted to delve into the subject of past lives were regarded in the same unfavourable light as 'witches', 'magicians', purveyors of 'black magic' and other unwholesome and disruptive elements whose unholy activities were strictly frowned upon by authority.

However, one cannot control experience, and records show that—in spite of the official teaching that a good Christian led only two lives (his life on earth and his life in the world to come)—many people over the years were convinced that they had lived before. The spiritual aspect of reincarnation—the fact that the cycle of birth and death and rebirth, like the cycle of the seasons, has a deep significance and meaning; that we are born, as Wordsworth phrased it: 'trailing clouds of glory ... from God who is our home'; and that we return to our origins at death—has been felt by most thinkers and intuitive, creative minds over the centuries. But, in addition to the theories, there have been various accounts of people actually claiming to remember a previous life, sometimes in great detail. The fact that many of them were inhabitants of far-away places like India or Burma meant that they did not on the whole make headlines in the west: the breakthrough here came in 1952 with the case of Bridey Murphy.

Under hypnosis a sitter can be regressed backwards, through the years of his present life to birth and beyond. The technique has been utilized in many of the medical and psychological treatments that have been developed during this century. When regressed to the age of (say) five, the patient will speak and behave as though his or her mental and physical age is in fact, that of a young child. As with *déjà vu*, however, other explanations may be given for this state of affairs, which dismiss claims that the person has actually 'regressed' at all.

But things that happened earlier on in this life can often be proved to have taken place. Evidence can actually verify the sitter's claim to have spent a night of trauma in a dog-kennel, alongside an astonished Great Dane, after becoming lost on holiday in Blackpool at the age of five—even if the sitter has completely forgotten the details until now. Recollections of clothes worn as a child, places visited, people known in the past, can all be confirmed by others who were present at the time. However, when the sitter regresses backwards beyond birth, to whatever sort of past existence presents itself, there can be, of course, no evidence of any kind.

Serious work has been carried out by some workers in this field to relate 'lives' to the historical past and to cross-check for historical accuracy. Anyone who makes a serious claim to be any well-known historical figure, for instance, would need at the very least to satisfy experts that their awareness of that person's life and times was unquestionably beyond mere scholarship.

Unfortunately, though, there are too many glib assumptions (even by some psychics) that one and one add up to three and a half. Some years ago I was talking to fellow-workers at a Psychic Fair on a quiet afternoon, and the subject turned to past lives. To my surprise, I discovered that I appeared to be in company that was far more distinguished than I had suspected. As the psychics spoke about their own past lives, names like Catherine the Great and Mary Tudor made their appearance.

In my own experience, this seemed most unlikely, but I did not question them. I said instead that I had always felt a great affinity for Anne Boleyn—and as a result had written a novel and two plays about her, involving a good deal of research—but that I did not think for a moment that I had actually *been* that wayward, difficult, tragic woman.

Irena, flashing-eyed and commanding, demanded whether I had ever suffered from throat problems.

'Why, yes,' I said, surprised. 'I had a terrible experience as a very small girl when my tonsils were removed. I've never forgotten it. And I feel difficulty in swallowing, often, for no reason. And a lot of sore throats.'

Irena was triumphant.

'That proves it. She had her head cut off, didn't she?'

It was a fascinating, if unexpected, suggestion, but I found someone else's theory that I had been 'not Anne, but very close to her, in her retinue' more acceptable. Even that, however, would never stand up under the sort of scrutiny one has to apply to the evidence when making any real attempt to deal with past lives.

For instance, in common with many women—writers and non-writers—I also feel great affinity with other historical characters: the Brontës, for example, and Mary, Queen of Scots, all of whom have appeared in novels and non-fiction I have written. Research and a writer's instinct for character—as well as perhaps the deeper awareness of the psychic— have meant that I can enter into the minds of such people and portray them convincingly, as many writers can. But this does not mean that I am the reincarnation of every historical personage in whom I have taken an interest. Other criteria must be applied, even if there can be no real evidence as such. Each person must, in the end, apply his own—and I believe always in the 'feel' I have mentioned before, the significance and rightness of the messages received from the past. To say that I was Anne Boleyn just because I am interested in her and have written work revealing that I know far more about her life than the average person would be utterly ridiculous.

My own personal conviction is that there is no real need to prove that past lives are historically accurate; it is like trying to hold the water or the wind in your hands. Practitioners vary so much in the way they work, and the results obtained can differ so widely, that the whole subject of past lives and ways of linking with them could not ever be satisfactorily categorized or classified. For instance, many cases of lives revealed under hypnosis give details of the subject's former name, the place where they lived and personal details about them. (It was this sort of case—that of Bridey Murphy—which first caught the attention of the general public in 1952.) Yet, when I link in to past lives for a sitter, I hardly ever get details of that sort; rather, I sense the emotional and spiritual state of the personality—who, nine times out of ten, would have been too uneducated or inarticulate (or too young) even

24

to be aware of the country in which it lived as a place with a name, or the year as one with AD or BC attached to it.

How can this be so? And why does the evidence that comes to me differ from evidence obtained by other people? My feeling is that each enquirer gets, as it were, what he deserves. Material about the spiritual and mental state of the personality comes to me because I am psychic and more concerned with the soul than the body. People who attempt an investigative, believe-it-when-I-see-it approach, will get the kind of details that might be obtained in a police interrogation. It is interesting that in many accounts of regression the subject seems dazed and cannot be very coherent. Because the questioners do not have the power to view them clairvoyantly, they are not given evidence of the sort which might come to me, of picking up the subject's inner feelings and emotions. Often these are unexpected and illuminating. It is important to bear in mind that, although concrete proof about previous existence would be useful, and would relieve the minds of many who find it difficult to accept the theory without proof, the concept of reincarnation is not really concerned with physical form, dates, names and places. It is concerned not with the body, but the spirit.

* * *

Almost everyone is capable of tapping this source, as it were, of spiritual awareness. A session I conducted with a group of visitors to a Psychic Fair recently involved ordinary people who had no previous experience of (and in some cases no particular interest in) actively participating in this sort of work. They were not devotees who had signed up for a Regression Session, nor were they especially interested in past lives.

I had been asked to give some sort of demonstration, and might well have given a talk, but felt compelled instead to conduct a short 'workshop'. There were some thirty to forty people sitting expectantly on the chairs in front of me.

'Before we begin, I must explain I propose to do a demonstration of past life regression,' I told them. 'I will regress you all—to whatever degree—to some past existence. You will be quite safe. Nothing frightening will happen. But in case any of you do not want to participate, please feel free to leave.'

'You mean we're supposed to have lived before?'

'You're going to go back in time?'

'You mean we will go back ourselves?'

There was a certain amount of doubt, confusion and hesitancy. Several people rose and withdrew, and then one or two others followed their example; most gave no reason for not wanting to take part.

'I will help you to relax under a light hypnosis—all of you, together—and take you back. You may experience nothing, but, again, please be reassured: you are quite safe; nothing frightening or upsetting will happen. But anyone who has doubts, or is not happy with the idea, please say so now.'

By this time, the numbers had gone down to about fourteen, and I asked those remaining to come forward and sit together in a little block in the first two rows of seats. When they had done so, I added a few more reassuring words explaining what it would feel like to experience trance—very relaxed, comfortable, fully aware of what was going on around them—and then I began to talk them into a relaxed state.

I was interested in them as a group, bearing in mind that they were simply 'members of the public', rather than psychic enthusiasts. Two adolescent girls who were sitting together found it difficult to enter the trance state: they were too 'jumpy' and nervous and, in the end, simply sat and watched. The others, to different degrees, began to show signs of being deeply relaxed.

'You are drifting back through the years of your life, letting go of the present. You will return safely to this moment and this place, feeling as though you have had a peaceful sleep. But allow your mind to drift back to the time when you were ten years old . . . six years old . . . three years old . . . allow yourself to drift

27

back to the time before you could speak or walk, when you were a tiny baby. And now you are drifting back even further, before you were born into your present life. Simply relax, feel safe and protected. There is nothing to fear. Allow yourself to drift back to a time before this, when you lived in another place and another body.'

I was watching them all closely, their breathing patterns and the position of their bodies as they sat with eyes closed, completely relaxed in their seats. But there was no sign of distress or difficulty, and I asked them mentally to look down at their feet in that past life, note what they saw, and then mentally inspect any clothes they were wearing or anything they noticed about themselves. The next step was to advise them that their feet would carry them along a passage to a large door. Reassuring them that it was safe to do so, I instructed them to open the door and note what lay beyond. And then I recalled them safely to the present and their own bodies, relaxed in their seats.

The results of this 'experiment' were interesting firstly because I was able to assess from a random group of people how easily they had entered the trance state. Only the two teenage girls had held back. The others had been excellent subjects, and several of them commented afterwards on how wonderfully fresh and free from tension they felt.

Out of those who had participated, at least

28

six said they had experienced nothing but some memories of their childhood and various 'flashes' that they did not think meant anything. One hardy ex-officer from the Army said he had found himself on a hill-top, which was very clear and vivid but which meant nothing to him. He declared with healthy scepticism that he did not think it proved he had had a past life at all—in fact, he did not believe in them.

But three people had something more positive to contribute. They had all 'gone back' to find they seemed to be in a different body to their current one. One woman described her arms as having been 'huge, with thick hair'. She told me: 'I think I was a man—or male, at any rate—and I was much taller and bigger, maybe nearly seven feet.'

The other woman in the group had also returned to a male body, and had found herself wearing shoes with buckles and white stockings. She could not remember any more than that, except a vague impression of walking on cobbles, though she emphasized that: 'The buckles weren't very smart, and I think I was poor.'

The last member of the three, a man, described himself as having been 'a woman, wearing something like a big white apron, very buxom.' He had managed to open the door and had found himself in what he thought was a kitchen—a huge, old-fashioned kitchen. He had felt at home, since he believed the woman had been a cook or upper servant.

Several of the others in the group had reached the door, but none of them had anything to report except the woman who had described her 'huge arms, covered with hair'. She had obtained a glimpse of what lay beyond and had been frightened by sensations of confusion and panic, dark shadows and unknown dangers. She had felt that a hostile world lay on the other side of the door and had proceeded no further.

It was interesting to observe that nothing that had happened during the experiment seemed to have made any impression on the participants. I did not attempt to explain, teach or apply what we had experienced to the lives of my sitters—after all, this was only a superficial demonstration. They seemed far more impressed by the relaxed result of the trance state.

* * *

After centuries of ignorance and terror, fearing the wrath of both state and church, educated and enquiring minds in the west led a revival of interest in the arcane and the occult (words which simply mean 'secret' and 'hidden'). Enquirers in the 1920s and 1930s found, to their gratified amazement, that they might well have lived lives in past times—often, by strange coincidence, as ancient Egyptian queens or

30

priests of Atlantis. Both of these historical periods are extremely common so far as past-life regression is concerned, and I personally often feel 'Oh, not *that* again' if I sense that a sitter's past life is emerging from either place. I am extra-vigilant and try to clarify details as fully as I can.

After a certain amount of frivolousness and plain fakery, as well as some genuine investigation and scholarship among enthusiasts, the subject of reincarnation leaped to prominence as a household word among the general public in 1952. This was the year of the celebrated 'case' of Bridey Murphy, in which, under hypnosis, an American housewife revealed the details of a past life as a nineteenth-century Irish woman, Bridey Murphy, giving names, dates and a wealth of authoritative background information that appeared to verify her story beyond all reasonable doubt. Although this caught the attention of the public, the Bridey case was not unique. There had been stunning instances of people remembering their past lives or regressing comprehensively to past existence before 1952. However, the case came to public attention at just the right time and in just the most spectacular manner. Details, including a runaway best-seller *The Search for Bridey Murphy* by the hypnotist involved, Morey Bernstein, were available to all. The veil of mystery was stripped away for good. After the outcry surrounding the case reincarnation would never again hover, mystically, as part of a dimly perceived religious faith—something beyond the comprehension or grasp of the ordinary mortal. After Bridey, everyone was free to participate in regression (or, in the jargon of hypno-psychobabble 'going back',) out of curiosity or just for the fun of it.

What many people do not realize, however, is that the soul commonly passes through more than one other life in its quest for spiritual enlightenment. Some authorities claim there is a more or less set number of lives per soul: fifty perhaps. Others envisage thousands of incarnations for each soul over millions of years of what we perceive as time. My own experience indicates that it is impossible to generalize; each soul is different, and specific knowledge of this sort is, in my view, something far beyond the capacity of the human brain to possess, wonderful though that brain may be.

Regression to one past life may be interesting and perhaps therapeutic but, more often than not, I have found that several lives need to be considered for the experience to be of any real use. It is as though the personality is like a jewel, cut with many facets: the details of one past life may reflect one part of the whole; a second will usually underline or add to the information being given. Sometimes I will link up with a third life, perhaps even a fourth. Occasionally I have found that lives do not come through to me singly. One young man had lived many lives, which I saw in a sort of drawn-out procession, but in none of them had he ever survived childhood. It was like looking at a line of small children standing close to each other—quick, brief lives of his spirit, recurring again and again, unable to break the chain and grow both physically and spiritually.

*   *   *

When I did a past-life session with Angie, she had already told me a little of her background in another connection. Not only could she remember a great deal about her past existence, she had also received corroborative information from other psychics, and she had clear recollections of herself as a young 'alien' on a spacecraft, travelling between Earth and her home in a far distant galaxy. She also informed me that she had been a Scots soldier killed in battle with the English. In yet another life, she said, she had lived in Atlantis.

When I began to link in with her past lives I made a conscious effort to clear my mind of the information I had been given. (It is fine to get 'proof' from different sources, but if I had linked in immediately to Scotland or Atlantis— or even to the 'alien' spacecraft—I would have been inclined to feel I might have been unconsciously influenced by what I had heard.) What did come through, incredibly powerfully, was the terror and thunder of a battlefield: cannon, gunfire, smoke. I picked up a young man, perhaps in his early twenties—a surgeon operating on the wounded in a makeshift hospital tent, under fire. Though it was difficult to be sure at first, I thought the year was about the mid-1800s, the place America at the time of the American Civil War. As the picture became clearer, I was able to see that the young man had been a Southerner, slender and fair-haired.

'You were in the middle of the war and the battle, but not a soldier,' I told Angie. 'You were a doctor, young, passionately dedicated, and you had perhaps only just graduated.'

As I concentrated on the figure of the young man, I could see that he had been comparatively sheltered, with little worldly experience. He had not been afraid; even amid the thunder of the guns and the screams of horses and men, he had worked, erect and tireless, far beyond physical exhaustion.

'But sometimes, you would go away to be alone, and you would be crying,' I told Angie. (The feeling I was picking up was so strong that my voice was difficult to control, and I had begun to weep soundlessly myself.) 'It was not from fear. They were tears of anger. You were filled with so much anger that these things could happen, and that you could do so very little. The wounded and the dying on every side broke you; it was like trying to stop the tide from coming in, and you felt your helplessness shaking your whole body like white-hot fury. I think you have lived on other battlefields before, there seems to be a sort of inevitability about it.'

Angie was looking at me sombrely.

'The other lives I was aware of were all earlier. I know I fought in battle many times, and when I died in Scotland, in battle, I swore I would never fight again.'

'No, you became a healer instead.'

'I am glad,' she said simply. 'Was this my last previous existence, do you think?'

I concentrated and after a moment, said: 'Yes, I think the way it came through, so clear and also so near, means you are still very close to it. I don't think you have experienced any other life in between.'

There were details to tell her about the young doctor who had been herself: his family and personality, and most interesting of all (for I do not usually get insistent details linking up unless they are important or significant in some way) the fact that he had been a virgin.

'That seems to mean something, but I don't know what,' I told her. 'We will probably find out as we go. It wasn't so much that he was physically a virgin, but that he was—well, spiritually a virgin, if you know what I mean. Sort of pure in spirit, unsoiled.'

Angie herself was in a relationship, so the physical symbolism was not relevant, but she said:

'I know. I think it's what I am struggling to achieve, that purity of the spirit. I understand exactly what you mean: I relate to him completely. And I am glad I was able to turn to healing. I am thinking of opening a Healing Centre—now, in this life.'

I knew she was psychic, but it came as something of a shock to hear that she was a trained Reiki as well as spiritual healer.

I linked into a second life, and this time I was not able to pretend the Scots connection was not there. It started off as a colour which swam vividly before me, the turquoise blue of a plaid, I thought, or of some battle flag or saddle cloth. I told her I could see her vividly.

'You were only young, in your late teens maybe, and sort of—well, the only word is callow. A bit of a country bumpkin, brown hair, pale and rather unprepossessing. Not really a foot soldier, just one of the "rabble" in a very fierce battle. I am seeing your death. It came from above and was very sudden, I think, so the man who cut you down was mounted, or else you were on the ground. There is this turquoise colour, which was something he was wearing, or which you could see, and in the rush I can make out clearly a sort of round shield, the type that might have been worn on the arm, quite small. The weapon was heavy, the blade went in—to the neck or shoulder, maybe—and that is it. You were gone.'

My impression was that the battle had taken

36

place round about the time of Robert the Bruce, and Angie told me she could remember her death, more or less as I had described it, including the turquoise colour and the shield. It was interesting that she thought she had been on horseback when the death blow had been struck, but I had seen the man who killed her on horseback, herself reeling below, and I felt very strongly that a gangling country lad, trailing along in the ranks, could not possibly have been part of a cavalry force. But it was not something to argue about. She remembered herself as that rather pitiful boy, and agreed with my description of him.

There was another small, but interesting difference in our accounts. I did not think the battle had been against the English; I thought the Scots had been fighting each other, and so it had been a Scot who had killed her.

'You were completely out of your depth: pure cannon fodder. You never struck a blow; you were just there and were killed. I think the weapon was a short blunt sword, or even something like an axe. It had a very thick heavy blade.'

'It was an axe,' she said. 'I felt it come right through and hit the front of my chest. I had a brother in that life—he is my spirit guide now—and I can remember I wanted him badly. The moment that I died, when my spirit rose from my body, was when I vowed I would never fight in battle again.'

I was able to detect from this life further confirmation of the 'virginal' state. The young Scots soldier had also been physically and spiritually untouched. I thought it seemed likely that Angie had been male rather than female in her past. She possessed the masculine strength rather than the feminine softness—but, in common with many spiritually advanced people, she had achieved in this life a balance of both which seemed to make her sex irrelevant. Once the spirit has left the body, sex as such ceases to exist, and in some incarnations one gains only an impression of different types of energy. This is particularly so when the lives in question are strange to us and different to the ones we are familiar with.

The third linking up that I did for Angie was to such a life. I had to concentrate for some time before I was able to begin putting it into words. Some images are difficult to describe, since there are no real words to use for them, and this was such a one.

'I can see figures, tall figures in some sort of white robes, standing on a flight of wide steps, but you were not one of them. They are standing, waiting. They are waiting for you, I think.'

Since I could not place the time, country or civilization, I felt it was important to describe them as fully as I could.

'They seem to be men, representatives of some sort ... and the place behind them is

38

vague, but it seems to be a kind of white stone-like temple or official building—though I don't think they were priests. I can't make out the length of the robes, but they wear headdresses of some sort, with curled pieces on either side of the head, linked up. It's not the shape of a crescent moon, but similar.'

Since I could not describe the headdresses to my satisfaction, I spent some moments trying to sketch the shape on a piece of paper, then continued:

'I don't know where you are in this landscape—it seems empty, apart from them and their building—but you are obviously here somewhere, or I would not see the scene. It seems like a very warm climate, some vegetation, and I can see a planet, or what looks like one, rising above the horizon, but it is much bigger than the sun, and a sort of silver-grey colour.'

'Maybe it was some place other than Earth,' Angie suggested. 'I know I have lived on other planets.'

I thought not, though I could not explain the strange 'sun'. Although there was an alien feel to the scene, I felt the men in their white robes were human, and of a high intelligence and culture. Still I could not find Angie's other self, but slowly I received a picture of something forming: a round object, similar to a diving bell or bathysphere, which seemed to be standing on the ground, propped up with several 'legs'

39

that stuck out of it at an angle.

I described it to her, adding:

'I don't know what it is. Except that it was not from outer space. More like from the sea, though I cannot see any water, and it doesn't look wet. But I think it was where you came from; you arrived in it. I sense you now, moving from it towards the group on the steps. I am seeing them through your eyes, I still cannot see who you were. One thing, though: you were important. They were important men themselves, leaders of their people, but they stood and waited for you; they knew you were coming. I feel you did not live in this place. You visited it, visited them, every so often, like a landlord visiting his property, making sure everything was in order.'

By this time, I was beginning to link in to Angie's other persona, but, as sometimes happens, it was so difficult to describe to her that I felt reluctant to do so in case the description seemed insulting or ridiculous. However, I had to be true to what my vision had given me.

'I think the time may have been some very early Atlantis-type civilization, and these men were highly intelligent, but you were something else altogether. I don't see you as a man or a woman; you were a sort of fish creature, a tall mass of jelly-like substance with long trailing pieces, like fins or seaweed. And I think you had only one eye, if that, right at the top. You

40

were incredibly superior to them. All conversation was conducted telepathically, and you had a fantastically powerful mind. Your people, whatever they were, lived somewhere else, but you visited the "outposts" of the empire every so often and made sure they knew who was boss. I don't think they liked you much—and you were so aware of your own mental superiority that you regarded them with contempt. I can feel your mind, and I have to say you were unbelievably arrogant. I think this past power and arrogance is what you have been paying for in your other lives. You needed to learn humility, how to serve.'

I felt we had as much of the answer as we could get in one session. Her refusal to relinquish her contemptuous attitude towards the rest of the world—springing from a natural superiority that had persuaded itself it had nothing to learn, and took everything for granted as its due entitlement—was one that I have come across quite often among advanced souls. They seem to have fallen, like Lucifer, into the trap of their own advancement and pride in very early civilizations such as Atlantis (and others which are not known to us).

Such souls are hampered by the fact that they actually were superior, intensely learned and gifted, often very spiritual. But they chose to make a god of ambition and power, lost their spiritual humility as a result, and struggled through difficult lives, achieving a great deal but unable to make the necessary submission of their egos to a higher power. Angie accepted my comments and said they made a lot of sense to her. When I remained unable to place the civilization we had seen in the last life, she suggested that the sphere might have come from Atlantis.

'Wasn't there a part of Atlantis under the sea? I might have lived there.'

'And the men in robes,' I said thoughtfully. 'They must have been on the surface, or else I would not have seen the planet in the sky. If it *was* a planet, and if it *was* in the sky.'

We had to leave it at that. But some time later I received two footnotes to this session. Angie mentioned casually that another psychic had told her she was 'surrounded by Incas'. I thought of the unusual headdresses I had not been able to identify. They had not reminded me of Inca headdresses at the time, nor had I thought of the men as Incas—they were too 'light', though whether the light effect came from their robes, their skin colour, or was just around them I could not tell. Yet the curled sides were very similar to Inca headdresses, giving the head a square rather than round silhouette.

She also told me she had begun regular work as a healer, and 'every time I approach the building where I work, I feel extremely medical. It just comes over me: the sensation that I'm not a healer, I am a doctor.'

When I contacted Angie to ask her permission to include her case history in this book, she informed me that she had recently been reading *Pleiadian Keys to the Living Library* by Barbara Mayciniak (Bear & Co, Santa Fé). In this the author gave details of extremely highly developed races of invertebrates and similar creatures (like fish) that existed prehistorically. They were thought to have had knowledge of DNA and conducted genetic experiments with human beings.

CHAPTER THREE

HOW DID I DIE?

The subject of past death is just as fascinating as past life, and the two threads are interwoven, often very closely. Mary, Queen of Scots—so famously executed at Fotheringay Castle on the orders of Elizabeth I—is forever associated with the phrase: 'In my end is my beginning'. This cryptic clue tells us a great deal about the significance of deaths that crop up in past-life sessions. Birth and death are more or less the same thing: gateways through which the soul enters the human condition and leaves it.

* * *

Carmel was a businesswoman in middle age, blonde, attractive, relaxed—somebody to be reckoned with. When I did a past-life session for her, I found that I got very little about how she had lived in the past, but a great deal of information on how she had died. The first life that came through was seemingly as much of a cliché as the ancient Egyptian queens and priests of Atlantis.

'You were thrown to the lions in a Roman arena. You died as a woman in your early twenties.'

As I linked up with her death, I described small details to her.

'There was a large group, standing on the sand, or whatever was underfoot. Some of the people were Christians, condemned for their faith, but there was none of that joyous singing and fixing their gazes on the beyond that is commonly imagined. Not on this occasion, anyway. The fear was terrible, something you could almost touch, and I have never really understood before exactly what the phrase "shit-scared" meant. I know what it feels like now.'

She was listening intently as I went on:

'I don't know where the arena was, but it was a big one. The scene is confused by the fear of death. The only two things I can clearly tell you are that you were so frightened you were hardly aware of anything, and you never even saw the lion or whatever it was that killed you. It was

44

over so quickly. Yet the amazing thing is that you were not there because you were a Christian—you didn't particularly believe in any faith—you were just difficult; you would not accept being told what you should think. You dug your heels in and refused to accept what you were told. You were prepared to go to that dreadful death just for the sake of your principles and your right to think for yourself.'

Carmel was smiling.

'That's me. I am like that now. I suppose I am difficult, and I must irritate others, but I do insist on making up my own mind.'

'A sort of Ancient Roman suffragette, an embarrassment to authority. I don't know what you did or did not do then, but you irritated someone in authority enough to die for it.'

I linked into another life, and found it came through quickly.

'This is awkward,' I told her. 'One cliché in the Roman arena, and now I have another: the French Revolution and the guillotine. This time you died as a young man, and, again, you were not there because you were particularly political. You weren't an aristocrat, either. You were, just like in the first life, somebody who would not shut up and kept embarrassing the authorities.'

'I can imagine that,' said Carmel calmly. 'And it's odd that you should mention the French Revolution and the guillotine. I get a weird feeling whenever there is any sort of

45

execution on TV, in a play or film. I feel really ill and have to switch it off.'

'That is because you were probably there,' I said. 'I think you were present at every kind of execution there was; you seem to have made a long career out of being executed because you would not be told what to think. It has happened over and over, not just these two times. Your tenacity has given you the great moral strength you possess in this life.'

* * *

When dealing with past-life sessions, the overall picture that emerges depicts a view of the subject of death subtly different from the one we hold in the western world today. For one thing, there seem to have been far more deaths. We do not realize, even when dealing with historical data, that every person who ever lived in the past also died, and often more brutally and painfully than they would today. The number of sessions in which the past life is of a child or young person who met an early death is very high.

Many of these young deaths include the victims of human sacrifice. In such cases, the 'life' includes very little apart from the death. I see this type of thing so often that, once again, I get that 'Oh no, not another one' feeling. Sometimes the child is thrown to sacred crocodiles, or other sacred creatures,

46

sometimes it is ritually slaughtered with a knife or ceremonial dagger. Invariably there is, in the link with that life, an uncomprehending, almost stupid, awareness of ceremony, great colour and rich costumes or trappings, feathers or beads, heavy robes to carry and something heavy weighing down the head. In most of the cases I have dealt with, the child, gorgeously dressed as it was led to its death, might well have been drugged, even anaesthetized, for there is little sense of struggle or real fear.

In one case, the man consulting me had been sacrificed many times over in different lives and had learned, through long experience, to be afraid, but mostly I do not sense fear or pain. Once in the crocodile pool, or whatever, death seems to have been swift and merciful.

These cases usually point to the sitters' endurance or lack of control over their destiny, something they need to struggle to turn into a positive virtue, rather than allow passively to rule them. Again though, one cannot generalize, and every death, like every life, is uniquely relevant.

* * *

Deaths in the past can linger into the present, often in sinister fashion. David's first 'life' came through slowly and was rather mystifying.

'I see a bridge, across water,' I told him. 'It could be anywhere in England . . . the water

47

sparkling fast . . . green grass, and I think a sort of mill-wheel or watermill. It seems like spring . . . blue sky, a general sense of well-being. But nobody is there. Does it mean anything to you?'

'I can recall a bridge,' he said, and I continued to concentrate. This time I picked up some sort of sulphur-yellow fog, hanging over water that was still and had a film of oil on the surface; the atmosphere was similar to that of an industrial city, with the shapes of buildings, warehouses perhaps, vague and lost in the gloomy fog. The scene was dark and unpleasant.

'There seem to be two bridges,' I said to David. 'Or at least, it might be the same one, but there are two sides to it, two views in opposite directions. One is the lovely, fresh, sparkling water tumbling over stones, and the other is this dreadful still pool, full of oil and filth. I don't know where either of the scenes are, but they seem to suggest Victorian England, or maybe even the Depression in the Thirties. I get the idea of Liverpool.'

David did not recognize any connection.

'At any rate, they are both completely empty, and that is the most important thing. You are not there, not on the bridge.' I paused to clarify my thoughts. 'Not your physical body, anyway. You committed suicide at this spot, went into the water. And what I am linking into is your spirit. You did not move on, you stayed here,

48

and your feelings and thoughts continue to go round and round in your mind, your memories of your life playing over and over, as they do—supposedly—at the moment of death. You have stayed there ever since and carried the situation with you into this life.'

The popular belief that the spirit of a suicide cannot rest has a good deal of truth in it. The act of suicide itself is not just a 'giving up' on the problems of life; it is an attempt to sidestep or avoid the spiritual lessons to be learned during the life-span prescribed for that particular incarnation of the soul. Consequently, the spirit must inevitably return to face the same basic lessons over and over again, until those lessons are accepted and learned, and the necessary spiritual progress has been made.

Speaking very broadly, cases of attempted suicide—which can be clinically described as attempts to obtain help in order to live, rather than serious attempts to die—have the effect of providing clear evidence for the survivor that suicide is not the answer. Having come through the trauma, they generally find they have acquired a certain amount of spiritual vision and are able to see that 'stop the world and let me get off' will not take away their inability to face up to it.

But attempted suicides are the ones who do not die. Genuine suicides—like David in his former life—seem to be motivated by isolation, intractability and a preoccupation with themselves. Suicide is a sad affair, but in many of the cases the people concerned have the opportunity to save themselves and, for whatever negative reason, choose not to do so. They will not recognize that there are other ways, that they are not an isolated island in a great universe; they will not see their sufferings are part of the universal suffering and can, with courage and acceptance, be overcome. Because of this lack of spiritual wisdom and refusal to try to achieve enlightenment, the suicide has made no progress in his life and remains 'earthbound', tied to the material plane. He must return and try again, until he passes this traumatic point safely.

I explained this briefly to David, and he accepted my words with a nod.

'Yes, I understand that.'

'You were a man in your early thirties when you died. The lovely springtime view from the bridge was your early illusions: how you wanted or expected things to be.' I continued 'But the yellow pool of oil was the depression, the disillusion: what went wrong in your life. I think the real trouble was that, though you had family ties—even a hard-working wife and children (a child who was delicate ... chest troubles, actually) and you had intelligence and skill at your work (some sort of book-keeping), you could not relate to the world at all, nor to the people in it. The more you tried, the more

50

isolated you became.

'In the end you simply wanted to get away from the reality because you could not accept it nor live in it. I feel you did not even have the ability to want anything any more. You were very tired. And because of your difficulties in deciding which way to go—whether to choose to face life positively or give up—you cannot leave the bridge. You are still on it, unable to make up your mind what to do.'

'It's strange,' David commented. 'I have often found myself standing on a bridge in this life, feeling paralysed, as though I cannot move. But it is all very true. I wonder . . . I can remember living as a fighter pilot. Was that before or after?'

When I linked in with a possible life as a fighter pilot, I could catch only a flicker, if that.

'If you were, I don't think there was much to the life except a death wish . . . perhaps an attempt to expiate what you had done by sacrificing yourself in war. But the personality seems very faint and non-existent. The gesture was not enough; the karma around you at the bridge might even have been building up from many previous lives. Whether you came back after the suicide or not, is not really relevant. It is this life that matters. You have come back very quickly to face it again, and you even have a full awareness of what the problem is.'

Together we discussed the problem as it had manifested itself in this life for him. He was an

51

extremely spiritual, psychic person, yet he had great difficulty in loosing the bonds of material things. Money difficulties were ever-present, and as soon as he dealt with one problem, two more arose.

'This struggle between your spiritual and material selves is like the two views from the bridge,' I said. 'But you do not seem able to let go of either.'

See-sawing between heaven and earth, he was constantly tired and wore himself out to no real purpose. I felt the trapped mind was still playing the same memory-tape, even in this life, and he agreed fully with my conclusions.

'If you can understand the problem and see that you have to make a decision and break the paralysis—rise above the lost state of suicide on the bridge—it should be easy. And yet, I can see it is not.'

'No, I try constantly to free myself,' he agreed. 'But I suppose because I got into it myself, I have to deal with it in my own way, and that might not be the quickest or the most obvious.'

Great wisdom there, I thought. Nobody can carry the karma of another, and something that one person could deal with easily might take someone else the struggle of a lifetime.

'It seems so sad though, for that man,' I commented. 'He just let everything go, it was a life wasted.'

David shrugged.

'Born in the wrong place at the wrong time,' he said.

* * *

Another such life—and death—was experienced by Rosy. In a relaxed state of regression she described the 'life' in which she found herself in medieval France.

'I am sitting on the grass, at the foot of a high stone wall, part of a tower. It is a château. The turf is green and beautifully tended.'

There was a curiously flat expression on her face and in her voice.

'Can you tell me what you are doing there?'

'Nothing,' she said blankly.

'Can you describe what you are wearing?'

'Heavy clothes, beautiful,' she said indifferently.

'What are you thinking?' as a grimace of distress touched her face.

She paused then said in a piteous, tiny voice: 'I can see everything, the grass and the sky and the sun. But I am not here—not really. It is as though I am in the wrong place; I do not belong. Everyone is very kind, but nothing touches me. As though something inside me is missing; as though I am dead, or was not really born.'

I picked up the feeling of alienation, of distance from reality and the consequent lethargy, the almost painful weight of the body and lack of interest in the mind.

'Are you ill? Perhaps paralysed in some way?'

'No. Just . . . not there. In the wrong place,' she added with doleful effort.

The next move was obvious.

'Then let yourself rest peacefully now, with no more need to worry. It is all over, there is nothing to worry about any more. I want you to move on to your rightful place—the place where you feel you should rightfully be.'

Rosy was silent for some time, then unexpectedly, her face lit up, losing the blankness that had been there when she spoke about her life at the château. She was somehow sharper, more defined.

When questioned, she revealed that: 'It is London in war-time.' She was a young woman in uniform and revelled in the dangers and the risks, feeling that, though a female, she was playing a man's part and living life to the utmost. She drove ambulances, she said, and liked dancing and was engaged. Even her manner of speaking had taken on the modernity of the twentieth century; it was so right it seemed to fit her just as the medieval life so obviously had not.

* * *

Experiencing the deaths of others in their past lives is usually like watching a film come to the end of a reel. The moment when the spirit actually leaves the body is a blanking-out—as though the end of the film had run from the reel, leaving the screen suddenly dark. Whatever happens to the soul after death does not register in my experience of past-life regression, save in exceptional circumstances, like those of David's suicidal earth-bound spirit. I simply say to the sitter: 'That was it. You were gone.' The body and what happens to it after death has occurred generally seems irrelevant. Sometimes, however, it plays a significant part in the on-going process of life around it, or holds some significance, and I may be shown what happens to it afterwards.

The case of Ivor was one such. I linked in to a 'life' which focused on his murder, or, at least, his death by violence.

'You were some sort of wise man or magician, living in a rather primitive community—it seems to be on the coast of Spain, maybe in the fourteenth or fifteenth century. It was poor and isolated, and you were feared by the other people because they thought you had strange powers—I think you were just more intelligent than they were. But what I am seeing is not your life but your death. Something killed you, and the people just got up one day and found you lying sprawled in the middle of their cluster of little huts.'

'What happened to me?' he asked with great interest.

55

I could not make it out, but I gave him the vision as I had received it.

'You were lying on your back, and your whole body, all down the front, was . . . well, sort of scraped bare. I have no idea what could have caused injuries like that. It doesn't seem possible. Nobody knew what had happened, but the mysteriousness of it frightened them, and they did not want to touch you to bury you.'

'Plague?' he suggested hopefully.

'No, it was actual injury, but . . . ,' I concentrated. 'The other thing I am getting is that you were attacked from the air. It was something to do with a UFO or some craft from space. But don't ask me what. Your death did become a sort of legend, though. The injuries just could not be accounted for. All down the front of the body, every inch of skin scraped red-raw.'

* * *

When witnessing past deaths, I may be shown happenings from different viewpoints. Changes of viewpoint seem to occur during the period of transition as the soul passes from body to 'out of body', and it is difficult to relate this to time as we know it. The process might take several hours, or just a few minutes.

Angie's second 'life' as the young Scots soldier was visible to me at first from his own viewpoint, looking out through his own eyes at

56

the man who was striking the blow that killed him. Immediately afterwards, however, when she was describing what she had felt and thought at the moment of death, I was looking down at the soldier from a point some way above him and a little to one side.

This happens often, and usually indicates the soul is departing from the body to hover above. Many people who have had so-called 'near-death experiences' have described how the spirit separates itself from the body as death is taking place, or when it seems death is likely to take place, and how they seem to be somewhere up on the ceiling, say, watching the surgeons and nurses and their own physical self in the operating theatre, or ambulancemen trying to revive them below on the ground after a serious crash. Jason's memory of the airship disaster also illustrates this process (though he did in fact die and his spirit moved on at that time).

There is another viewpoint from which the death may be viewed, which is even more subtle. Apart from seeing the scene through the eyes of the person concerned (or, as in Jason's case, through the eyes of the departing spirit), I may see it from a completely detached point of view, usually from the side and a little above. It is not always easy to identify which is which, especially if the death is quick.

Sometimes the soul returns to the physical body, which then recovers. When dealing with past lives and past deaths, I can only go as far as the transitional stage. I do often see the scene from the viewpoint of the spirit, but I can never see what takes place afterwards—once the soul has actually left the earth and has been released from the human condition. Interestingly enough, however, I can make contact with departed souls in my work as a medium. In my experience, though, the spiritual world has its own rules, and one has to abide by them; it is impossible to work on all the planes at once. If I am working on the earthly plane of this life and past lives here, everything I am shown will be largely concerned with earthly existences. Thus, once I am shown a spirit departing for another plane, I cannot follow it.

* * *

There is a saying that a good Christian should try to live his life with his deathbed in mind. In just the same way, true spiritual awareness indicates that a successful existence in the present can be achieved by applying the lessons to be learned from the deaths of the past.

Fiachra, a blue-eyed, raven-haired Irish girl, was stunningly beautiful and successful. Yet when I linked up for a past life, I found something surprisingly tragic.

'Whoever or whatever you were, you were

58

blind,' I began. 'I see nothing. There is no awareness of sight. And you might have been deaf also.' I stopped to clarify my impressions. 'I get the feeling, too, that you were crippled in some way; you were unable to move.' At last I had the picture. 'I can't tell you where or when, but you existed as a person—just a young baby, I think . . . could have been male or female, I have no means of knowing. You seem to be close to the ground somehow, just sort of lying there. You had no arms or legs—I get the feeling it was because of a drug, the Thalidomide type of thing—and you could not see or hear. I have no sense of pain, but also no sense of connection with the world or other people. Isolation is almost complete. I think you lived a short time, a couple of years at the most, then died very young.'

Fiachra was able to identify with this sense of isolation and helplessness, since she had suffered abuse as a child, and was still trying to recover from the emotional scars. I went on to another life.

'I get two sorts of glimpses,' I told her after I had concentrated hard. 'They are only glimpses. Both children: one standing on a long flight of marble steps, out of doors, perhaps in Rome; the other hiding under a fruit bush, the type of bush you would get in an orchard or kitchen garden . . . in England. But I can't tell you the period of either. I feel something came to both these children—an accident or death.

Again, there is no sense of identification with the world or people around. The sensation is sort of frozen, icy, as though held under some sort of spell. They were both female I think, maybe two, three years old.'

I examined the pictures I had been given.

'You seem to have been unable to relate to life. In fact, I get the feeling you almost willed yourself dead. You did not want to live.'

'That phrase describes it exactly, under a frozen spell,' she said. 'I have always felt like that. I feel as though I carry a huge weight of sadness with me, but I don't know why.'

'We are all shown our lives before we are born, and agree to accept them,' I told her. 'But it is as though you said you would come, and then turned away each time you were born and refused your life once you were here. You have never come past the first few years, except of course now.'

'Well, in this life I was born with a serious heart condition,' she said unexpectedly. 'I had to undergo a big operation at four-and-a-half. If it had not been done I would have died when I was twelve.'

This was really interesting.

'So in this life you had a choice too,' I said. 'You could have chosen to refuse to live, and died once again as a young child. The pattern would have been the same. I think you did actually make the choice to live at four-and-a-half, when you were undergoing the operation;

60

you chose to accept this life and the lessons you need to learn from it. Did you have any experience which might reflect this? Anything you can remember?'

'No, I can't remember anything about the operation,' she said. 'Just this inexplicable, dreadful sadness, and . . . a very great lack of confidence.'

'Emotionally, you are probably still four-and-a-half,' I told her. 'You took the life, made a great effort, but you still do not really want to be here, do you?'

She considered, then shook her head with a half-mocking, half-desperate little smile.

'No. I don't.'

* * *

Deaths in past lives take place as a very natural process. Sometimes the innocence and purity of the spirit which is departing mean that the passing is very much a going home—even when the death may be from violence or some form of struggle. Purity, faith, trust and acceptance, however intuitive, make death a joyful return, rather than a sad and fearful journey. In my experience, the deaths of animals fall into this category, and it is rare to find animal spirits that are 'earthbound'. If they are (and I have dealt with several cat and dog 'ghosts'), it is for some reason other than difficulty in accepting death.

61

One elderly cat, Baggins, still lurked after death in the passages of the house where he had lived, so that the family kept falling over him, but it was lack of strength that had kept him there. His death had caught him unprepared, and when his former mistress was directed to 'see him home' and consciously help him to depart from this world, she was able to watch his spirit make its purposeful way down the stairs to the front door, which had been left open at my instruction, and be gathered lovingly into the light that waited. Other pets return to give reassurance and comfort to their owners. Their motive is always pure devotion.

*　　*　　*

The fear of dying, which is often confused with a fear of death itself, is a vital part of the human condition. In the same way that Carmel was 'shit-scared' as she stood in the arena waiting for death to come padding towards her on tawny paws, so Angie, in her life as the young Scots soldier, was so terrified at the battle raging round her that she was literally too paralysed to move. Even I, who have, so to speak, witnessed and experienced the sensation of death at second hand hundreds of times over, cannot honestly claim that I contemplate my own in a completely serene manner. In the same way that all human beings, when they are born, know they must breathe in order to live, so they are programmed also to cling to their human condition until the last possible moment.

And each death in the past has its own message, its own significance, however seemingly meaningless or futile. Many of the 'lives' I have linked into have been comparatively trivial. Some spirits are still new, just beginning to learn, perhaps even unaware of the spiritual. Jacinth, an unassuming housewife in her forties, had had several such lives.

'I get a sensation of a girl: an ordinary peasant-type girl, nothing very special ... vaguely medieval or earlier. She is crawling under some sort of wooden building on her hands and knees. There is something very wrong. I think she is ill, hardly aware of where she is or what she is doing. There are other shapes there, bodies lying, but it's difficult to make out if they are dead or alive. Well, they will all be dead soon. It is some kind of plague.'

She felt that, simple though this image seemed, she could identify quite strongly with the young girl, lost, ill and trying to cope as best she could.

'And all the time,' she added quietly, but in a tone that came straight from her heart, 'all the time knowing, being afraid that whatever I do, it won't be enough. I'll never manage, never win—and I don't even know what the battle is all about.'

Then we tried a second 'life'.

'A child ... maybe five, but seems much younger because it is painfully thin, a bundle of sticks. I think it is a boy. It is crawling under some big leaves, something like rhubarb leaves, only much larger. There are bits of vegetables rotting in the ground, and the child is trying to find something to eat. It is covered with dirt and scabs, no clothes. It cannot walk; the legs drag behind, the bones are twisted and too weak to take any weight. It is all alone; everyone else and everything else gone. It is dying of starvation.'

Such apparently small tragedies, which may only seem to form a background to the more spectacular 'lives' of great spirits that are advancing along the path to enlightenment, are just as important in their more modest way. Jacinth had suffered and sought in the past, nameless 'lives' lost in the unstoppable and ruthless advance of human history, and indeed the progress of nature itself. But in this life she was able at last to become aware of the spiritual truths she had searched for so long to find.

'It is like discovering water in the desert,' she said, smiling, as I brought her session to an end. 'Food for the soul. I feel I struggled through a lot to get here, but ... well, just the glimpse I am having now of how *big* it all is, makes me feel incredibly powerful and strong. I mean, there isn't really any battle, is there? In the end, everything is a part of living, and, when you look at it like that, death really doesn't matter at all.'

CHAPTER FOUR

THE GREAT AMONG US

I have never felt free to say categorically to any sitter 'You were Joan of Arc', or 'I'm sorry to have to tell you that you had a past life as Attila the Hun' or 'Vlad the Impaler'. As I have mentioned previously, very few famous people emerge during past-life sessions, and, even when they do, I do not feel it would be accurate to tell them 'You were so-and-so'. Instead, I say 'I sense an energy that is similar to my picture of so-and-so.' In some cases, my cautious presentation has been met with a quiet nod from the person concerned, who was already fully aware of his previous identity.

The truly great among us know who they are, and they do not need recognition from the media, nor monetary incentives to 'tell their story', nor appearances on breakfast television. In my experience, they are always the last people one would expect, at first glance, to be 'great souls': a little odd perhaps, different, but quiet, self-contained and unspectacular. In nearly all the cases I have dealt with they are riddled with emotional problems and self-doubt.

There is all the difference in the world between the delusions of schizophrenia and the awareness of its own identity that a great soul possesses. Few, if any of the truly great will reveal themselves to others. If a clairvoyant like myself becomes aware of their real nature, they will admit it, and even discuss it, but it is not obvious in the normal course of everyday living. The great are not paranoid, and they do not judge themselves or suffer from undue feelings of guilt, even though they are generally struggling hard to keep their footing on the material plane, while all the time they long to return to higher realms.

* * *

I had known Rob for about a year, and appeared with him at psychic events. He and his wife Vanda sold New Age crystals, tapes, books and other items. Vanda was graceful with waist-length, dark hair and dark eyes, friendly and easy to speak to. Rob, at first, used to keep very much to himself, and it was not until I discovered they were going through a rocky patch in their marriage, and Vanda spoke to me about her troubles, that I came to actually sit down and talk face-to-face with Rob.

He had agreed, at Vanda's suggestion, to

66

have a session of clairvoyance with me, in the hope that it might help to sort out their difficulties. We took half an hour off from the business of the Psychic Fair and went out of the hotel where it was being held into the grounds. There were lawns, a seat under a shady tree, with a fountain playing into a pool of ancient and deeply brooding goldfish beneath waterlilies. It was high summer. For the first time, as we spoke, I felt Rob's personal strength of character, but at the time I was mainly concerned with helping them to each communicate their private hurts and lower the defences that were keeping them apart. Both were afraid to show their real feelings, in case they were further hurt. Rob spoke to me honestly, however, and I was impressed by the previously unsuspected depths of his personality.

They managed to work things out between themselves, and it was not until some weeks later that Rob and I actually settled down to do a past-life session. I knew he was psychic (as was Vanda): I had glimpsed his quiet power, but he was still very much his own person, and I was interested to see what might emerge as I linked into his first 'life'.

'This is quite complicated,' I told him. 'I see a city in flames, at night; the flames are roaring and making everything red, and you are on a bridge across a river—a reasonably big river, the water streaming red from the fire. You are

67

helping people, women holding babies and children, to cross to safety. The crowds are terrified; they are desperate to cross the bridge. You are a young man—twenty, say—and at first I thought you were some sort of evangelical convert of the Methodist era; you wear plain white shirt and dark breeches, with your hair, which is dark, tied back at the back of your neck. The scene looks earlier than that, though, more like the Great Fire of London.' I paused, thoughtfully. 'I suppose there were other fires in other cities at different times, but this is certainly a bad one.'

Rob was listening with interest, and I proceeded.

'It's not the scene that is important here, though. This young man was—well, without offence, I can only use the word pure. He was "given to God", as one might put it, and really genuinely in touch with his God. Nothing else mattered to him. He gave himself to others; he poured all he had out to them without asking for anything back. He was incredibly at peace with himself. And he didn't need anybody. He was sort of like a living likeness of light and power. I have never come across anyone so removed from human weaknesses and so spiritual. He just shone with complete purity. Are you aware of anything like this within yourself now?'

Rob did not hesitate. There is no place for false modesty when working clairvoyantly, since the clairvoyant can see the truth.

'Yes,' he said quietly.

I was examining the situation further.

'I thought at first he had had some experience on an evangelical level and been converted, but maybe he just . . . knew?'

'I have always known,' Rob said softly. 'I didn't find it easy to accept, but it has always been there.'

'He was alone, this young man. You are too, in spite of your family, aren't you? You have to be, I think. You are just—isolated by what you are.'

'Yes,' he agreed.

'And it is interesting that, although he is helping the people across the bridge, it is in a detached way, I mean, he does not know the people. It was out of great compassion towards humanity in general, rather than getting close to them. He did not find it easy to be close to anyone, though he might well have died for them. You have the same problem now.'

Rob nodded.

'The significance of the bridge is striking too,' I continued. 'As though he was helping to guide souls from turmoil and darkness and pain to where they would be safe. The instinct was to minister, to guide and show the way. He knew that was his life's work. Can you relate to it?'

'Very much. I am working to develop my psychic and spiritual powers. But I doubt myself. I haven't the confidence.'

'There is something even more significant about this scene. The young man—you—were in the middle of the bridge. When the crowds had gone, when everyone was safely across, you remained there, you did not follow them. It is as if you did not belong in either place: neither where the flames were burning nor the safety of the other bank. You are isolated here, belonging nowhere. Left alone. No one came to look for you. It is almost as if you were detached from the human race. You don't follow the same rules of existence. I think you feel this now, you feel the loneliness and it's almost unbearable.'

'It's true,' he admitted quietly. 'I feel so detached I can't make any contact with anyone at all—within myself, I mean. I can love my family, but I am cut off from them. It is . . . very difficult, like a burden I have to carry.'

'It is always more difficult for strong, advanced souls,' I said. 'They cannot lean on others, they have to walk alone. Let's try another life, and see what we get.'

A sunburst of colour resolved itself into the dancing, interweaving shapes of birds, scarlet and gold feathers gleaming in sunlight, hopping and darting about the confines of a huge and fantastically constructed cage.

'They are glorious, like jewels,' I told Rob. 'I don't know what sort of birds, but they have long feathers, and tufts up over their heads.

70

They seem to be in a type of ancient Japanese or Chinese courtyard or garden, and there is sunlight and a blue sky. The scene is utterly lovely, but it seems to be empty. I cannot see any human being; there is nothing there except the birds.'

I asked Rob whether the birds meant anything to him, but he shook his head. I concentrated harder.

'No, there is nobody there, just the birds. I can see another scene overlaying this one though. The colours are incredibly beautiful, blue and green. Looks like more birds—peacocks, I think. Their tails are shining in the sun, and there is grass around, a wide lawn. I'm looking for a gardener or someone, but this is empty too. There is no cage, but grassy terraces, and a high wall around the edge, like a castle wall, stone, very old.'

Still Rob could make no sense of the visions.

'You could have been a bird,' I hazarded, 'but I don't think that is the answer. I can see so many. And it seems to be symbolic that, although they are free and can fly about, or walk about like the peacocks, they are not really free at all. They cannot get out of the cage or beyond the wall. Beneath all that beauty there is a great sadness.'

'I know what you mean,' he said quickly. 'It's like the other side of situations that are beautiful being . . . well, heart-breaking.'

I felt that the life with the birds symbolized

71

the struggle that Rob had had in the past to accept different realities, to achieve harmony and balance in the face of extremes of polarity.

'The man on the bridge only accepted life insofar as he did not actually have to take part in it. He laid down his own rules, as it were. He gave, but it was what he chose to give—not a submission, a giving without conditions. And he was unable to take. Your soul has come a long journey, and you do not want to descend to the seemingly petty and mundane level of the rest of humanity. You have seen what it is like to really fly, to be free of the cage, and you long all the time to escape the confines of human give-and-take.'

Rob nodded his understanding.

'You have long since learned all the lessons, and, though you would like to stay in the higher realms where you belong, you come and struggle here on the earth to give the help that only you can give,' I said.

I was certain by this time that in Rob I was dealing with a very great and advanced soul. As often happens in this sort of case, he seemed to understand telepathically everything I said before I voiced it, and I knew what his feelings were before he expressed them in reply.

'I feel I must stay here, but—you are right—I have to struggle to make it work,' he said, and there was great sadness in his voice. I felt as though the scene with the birds, beautiful though it was, underscored his loneliness and resignation like a mournful dirge, a gorgeous lament filled with desolation. I linked in to a third life.

'Even then, you were a great leader, a wise adviser to your people,' I reported. This life had taken place somewhere in Central America—which is often the setting for past existence because of the great civilizations which flourished there for so long. Many of the lives lived there in Aztec, Mayan and other eras were extremely spiritual and meaningful.

I saw Rob as a man possibly in his sixties, short and slightly built but very erect, and with dignity around him like a cloak. An ascetic and spiritual person, with a mind as translucent as clear water.

'Unfortunately, you could not accept the day-to-day activities on a human level then either,' I told him. 'I see a sort of frenzy of material living, human sacrifice and a lot of overindulgence going on in one of the cities— Aztec perhaps. Low, dark stone corridors and rooms. A lot of gold, yelling and half-naked bodies. Torches burning. Blood. You were disgusted; your fastidious soul was so revolted you could not stand it. The people did not want to listen to you.'

'I can take that,' he nodded, a shadow crossing his face. 'You simply turned your back on them all,' I told him. 'The burden was too much. I see you turn and walk straight out of the city, or whatever it was, and up a path—a

73

sort of hill track—that went through a lonely, bare landscape. You took nothing with you, and you never looked back. There was a high mountain in front of you, and you carried on following the path upwards. The sky was very blue, the place very high, the air like crystal. At the top, where the mountain flattened out, there was a wide lake, silvery-grey, with small reeds or sedges in clumps at the edge. It stretched as far as you could see. It had no waves, but rippled all over very gently. I see you just standing there, looking out across the lake, alone, your back turned on the rest of the world. Whether you ever returned to the city, I can't tell.'

It was obvious that Rob's spiritual problem—his disgust with and distrust of the human condition—went very deep and had been with him for many lifetimes. But I did not realize just how a great soul may suffer from its own greatness until the last life I linked in to for him.

After holding his hands and concentrating, I looked straight into his face.

'I don't know how to tell you this, but—I get a most powerful presence, awesome, incredibly strong and magnetic, and yet filled with human anger and anguish. Rob, without any doubt you have lived as a man of the stature of the Biblical Moses.'

I watched his impassive features. There was no need for him to say anything.

'You knew.'

'Yes,' he said.

'It was the same pattern, great spirituality and qualities of leadership, but your people turned to idle frivolity and materialism. The vision I had was as Moses came down from the mountain with the tablets of stone and found the Children of Israel worshipping the Golden Calf. An intense sense of bitterness and rage which you must somehow overcome. But, Rob, if you were great enough to live as Moses, what on earth—literally—are you here to learn now?'

We concluded that, as with many great souls, too disdainful to descend to the human level, Rob was here in this life to learn how to share himself with others as a human being, and to appreciate what they had to offer him. He needed to be able to join in as part of the merry-go-round, not control it or hover fastidiously some distance away.

As we finished the session, I asked how and when he had come to be aware of the Moses persona. Its powerful energy had staggered me, but he spoke of it with calm matter-of-factness.

'Right from when I was a child, that story always gripped me: the bulrushes, the whole thing, but mainly the famines and plagues, knowing what it had been like to lead the people out of Egypt, the parting of the Red Sea—so many great miracles. But it wasn't just miracles, there was pain and anguish—I felt I

75

knew their pain.'

'Yet you are not a Jew,' I said. 'Do you identify with them strongly in some way?'

'I feel great sympathy with every religion. They persecute each other—they love their god yet they fight and kill in the name of that love. Somebody said: "People don't need gods, gods need people." Look at ancient Egypt; there were so many gods, yet each was only as strong as the number of followers. We all have our own perception of God, but in the end they are one and the same.'

As I nodded my agreement, Rob added:

'I feel I am here just to spread that message, and that the God who called me in Egypt is the same one who calls me now.'

* * *

Another unexpected revelation arrived at the end of a long evening at another Psychic Fair. I was tired and did not want to do any more sittings, especially as the young man who presented himself seemed the most unlikely material with which to work. He was slight, very nervous and Chinese. I could not even be sure at first whether he understood the English words I spoke to him. But he was genuinely in need of help, and I agreed to give him a past-life session.

As I held his hands I picked up a deepening sense of his terrible fear. He was shaking with it, and when I questioned him about the cause, he told me he did not know what to do with his life, how best to use it for the benefit of humanity. He could not see his way; his doubts were racking him. Should he go into a monastery, he wanted to know, retire from the world and devote himself to prayer? Or should he pursue his intellectual studies as a student and get a job?

Linking in to his past lives, I found to my surprise that I linked in with immense spiritual energy and power. But, great though his spirit undoubtedly was, the first two lives I described to him displayed the same characteristics as his present life.

'In the past,' I told him, 'you were just as afraid, hated being part of this world just as much as you do now. I see you somewhere in North America or Canada—the far north—surrounded by pine-covered mountains, thick vegetation, lakes, streams, nature. You were a young man who chose to live alone, not just a trapper or that kind of person, you actually cut yourself off from human contact and lived simply, like a hermit, dwelling in the spiritual realm. You were not a medicine man, and you did not try to do anything with your spiritual power, which increased all the time.' I shrugged. 'You just lived like that, cut off from everyone else, until eventually you died.'

I was trying to calm and reassure my sitter, to still his furious agitation. I found it strange to equate his thin, nervous appearance with the great strength and power I found hidden within.

'You know about your power,' I told him. 'That does not frighten you. What does is your terror of the world and having to exist in it. You want to escape, just as you did when you lived in the far north, don't you? It is not just a longing for meditation and a desire to dedicate yourself to God—or whoever—that makes you want to run to a monastery. You have already passed that spiritual landmark.'

He was able at last to express his thoughts and feelings, and he told me that he thought he needed instruction badly. He felt unable to make decisions and cope with his future. He felt completely vulnerable and did not know how to protect himself.

I linked in to another life and found almost exactly the same picture. A youth in a remote place, choosing to live alone cut off from all human contact, never speaking nor hearing another human voice for his fifty-odd years of living. It was little wonder that in his present life he stammered and stuttered and had great difficulty in putting his words together or conducting a conversation. And yet, beneath it all, there was still the wonderful, incredible great soul, centuries old in power and wisdom, so pure that I felt in awe of it as I sensed it communicating with me.

'Your problem is rather obvious, isn't it?' I

smiled, and he grinned rather jerkily back. 'You shouldn't be here really, you should be with angels or other elevated beings on some very high plane. You feel uncomfortable in a human body, you want to give to humanity but without having to get too close to human beings. I think you have run away every time you could in the past. This time, perhaps you will learn to have confidence in yourself and, I suggest, don't run away to your monastery too soon. Try facing the world first; the monastery will always be there, you know, and you can take "retreats" to keep yourself going without making a life-time commitment.'

He was looking a little brighter. 'That makes some sense,' he nodded.

'It is not just the spiritual part of you that matters, the wonderful shining soul I can see, and which you are sharing with me now, giving *me* upliftment and healing and power,' I pointed out. 'Everything else about you is just as important, just as vital to the world. Your learning and the degree you will obtain, the position you will take up. You might be the man to discover a cure for cancer or to touch other people's souls through painting or poetry. Your potential is limitless.'

This gave him food for thought, and I suggested we tried one more 'life' before his session ended. I knew the soul was a great one, but the vision that came to me still took me very much by surprise.

'I am getting something quite different to the others. In this life you were almost the complete opposite to those wilderness types. You lived in Europe, and you were a musician—a pianist—a great pianist.' The images did not go away, they recurred with increasing urgency. I lowered my sitter's hands and looked at him.

'I think . . . I cannot get away from the name and energy of Mozart.'

He shook his head in dazed wonder. 'I have no idea how to play the piano. I never learned.'

'It's the energy, the powerful energy which I feel, not the musical ability,' I told him. 'As though all the power concentrated in you threw you into a life which was frantic, more difficult to cope with than the withdrawals into the wilderness because you could not escape from it. There seems to be a sensation of manic flinging yourself at the boundaries of living. I feel this man, too, tried to escape, but he could never get away from himself, and he was driven by his powers and ability. He had little control, he was never at peace with himself, and could never rest. It is possible it was some other great musician, but the raging, raving energy of genius that I feel is Mozart.'

* * *

Sometimes the persona may identify itself in a more prosaic manner, with less flamboyance.

80

The power that I feel can range from dramatic explosiveness to quiet subtlety, depending on the character and personality of the individual with whom I am in touch.

Jeff was psychic, and I already knew he had great personal presence and power, so I was not surprised when, on holding his hands to link in, I saw an image of red—the colour of poppies—which then darkened to give me the vision I described to him. I felt immediately that the identity of this previous existence was very clear, but—because it was likely to be the most commonly known name in this connection—I did not reveal it.

'I get a Cardinal, in medieval times—Italy, Spain or else France. Did you know you had been a Cardinal?'

He nodded, unsurprised.

'Do you know which Cardinal?' I asked, blanking off the name I had in my mind while I waited for him to answer.

'Richelieu. There is the link with my name, [Richards],' he said. 'It's practically the same.'

This was what I had felt too, but I had an almost disinterested overview of the man in later life: very thin, slight, intensely capable. It was almost as though the vision was not interested in his worldly achievements. And the red stain, the poppy colour, seemed to be far more significant.

'I think there was a great difference between his later life and when he was a boy—a young man,' I said. 'I have a picture that is very clear ... of his young self—maybe in the middle or late teens—at a time when he was already studying for the Church, though I'm not sure in what way exactly. He is in a dark place ... might be a church or some sort of church property ... he is dressed in a darkish blue flat hat and short robe or tunic. He is nothing like his gaunt, slight build of later years, he is—well, the word that comes into my mind in every sense is "blubbery". He is crying bitterly, and his plump body is shaking. I think he was raped, and by other men—maybe other clergy. I get the sensation of penetration into the back passage, and it was very painful. The poppy colour was the blood.'

I asked Jeff whether the experience had ever occurred in his own life, or meant anything to him, and he reluctantly answered:

'No—not a thing.'

I was concentrating.

'Definitely something like this took place. He might even have been raped with some sort of metal instrument. It was very traumatic, and there was a lot of blood. But what this pathetic creature has to do with the cool Cardinal he became, I don't know. The picture is very clear, though.'

I felt there was little sense of balance or control in Jeff's character. He could rise to greatness, and possessed all the potential—yet, as I had previously observed, there seemed to be something holding him back, some point beyond which he could not pass. As Richelieu, he seemed to have been able to achieve his full potential, yet the blubbering youth crying in the dark of the gloomy vaulted church or hall, or wherever he had been, seemed a phantom that might well have haunted him for the rest of his life.

Jeff agreed that there did seem to be a point he could not pass, and asked almost desperately:

'How can I learn to let go and move on?'

'You might well be still working out some heavy karma. You're trying, that's the main thing. You're taking steps, even if they seem to be very small ones. You are making real progress, even if you don't think so. The main thing is, don't give up. Keep on trying, and do your best—that is all anyone could ever ask of you.'

* * *

NATAL HOROSCOPE CHART: ARMAND-JEAN DU PLESSIS, CARDINAL ET DUC DE RICHELIEU

Date of birth: 13.9.1584. Place of birth: Poitou, France. Chart by Richard Lawler, Astrologer. Commissioned by Dilys Gater for comparison with the past-life evidence for Jeffrey Richards.

Richelieu's Virgo Sun causes him to contemplate perfection. His analytical traits bring a discrimination to file his visions and work hard while waiting for the moment. Despite his expensive clothes, he was often modest in other ways.

Health-wise, typical of Virgo, digestive problems were such that he had some difficulty with assimilation of food and the resulting bowel complaint (possibly gluten sensitivity) would have caused bloat and blotchiness. [In response to my pursuing this subject] The enemas of those times would have been painful, as instruments were very primitive, and undergoing medical attention could have caused trauma.

Enormous creative energies were such that his self-imposed schedules often weakened him. His tolerance could give way to sublime passion for his values.

His Moon indicates his mother being the strong influence that saved his family fortunes but chose his profession for him. He took to his career (in the Church) and was an able administrator, often sensitive to the needs of his countrymen for tangible as well as spiritual values.

His wealth and position was used to uphold his principles, which upset the more corrupt officials and politicians around his territory. His influence was wide—he had the ear of the highest representatives of spiritual and temporal power.

He could be totally goal-orientated, looking forward to the next challenge, but he could also be a cold opportunist who sought out the most advantageous links. He was crafty, but could suffer from broodiness when his path ahead was impeded.

His sharp mind could decipher the flaws in others' thought and character. Today he could have been a teacher, social worker, politician or environmentalist.

He used unusual patterns of speech to entreat and persuade others; all fell victim to his boyish charm and style of dress. He inspired respect, rather than warmth or friendship, and did not hesitate to use the ideas of others as well as his own to his advantage. His apparent frankness hid a complex personality made up of paradoxes.

*   *   *

The interpretation of the impressions I receive as part of a 'life' may be inaccurate, because of my human fallibility, yet corroboration can nevertheless come from unexpected sources. However, in this case there is no way, short of interviewing Richelieu or his personal physician, in which real evidence could be obtained about the nature of the violation of the body that I picked up.

All forms of corroborative documentation,

opinions and theories must be carefully considered, and it is up to the individual to weigh the evidence and make up his own mind.

CHAPTER FIVE

TIME, *BARDO* AND THE CASE OF GERRY M

It should by now be obvious that there is far more to the subject of past lives (reincarnation) than a few interesting hoppings in and out of other bodies, or even identification with past traumas, and the ability to apply the relationship to problems in the present. The concept is immense, cosmic, and a proper understanding requires a lifetime's serious study, awareness of the experience itself, and a willingness to expand the mind and learn, even if it means moving into high, mystical realms of thought.

For some, the spiritual and mystical aspects are things they do not—at present—want to contemplate seriously. But, even if one can accept the idea of past lives—of the fact that we may have occupied other bodies in different times and places—and even if we accept that there is some sense in the idea that it might all be in order to develop the soul and lead it out of the darkness through enlightenment, it is not surprising that there are many other questions that people repeatedly ask.

In the immense spiritual concept these are trifling matters, but they worry the practical mind that cannot see with cosmic vision or even with trust and faith. People want to know whether their loved ones who have 'gone to a better world' are still there and able to be contacted, or whether they have been born in another body and become somebody else. They become distressed because they think they might not recognize their parents when they themselves die and join the rest of their family in that shining country.

They ask why they, or other members of their family, are suffering pain, loss and distress in this life. 'If we were given a choice before we were born, why did we choose to hurt ourselves like this?'

They do not care for the idea that they will, after death, become 'somebody else'. 'How can I still be me if I turn into a man? I don't want to be somebody else.'

Many other fears and worries, probably so difficult to express that they cannot be formulated, remain unspoken. But the reason for all of them is basically the same—that they are concerning themselves with the mechanisms, rather than with the concept itself. And the concept of past lives, reincarnation, is at once extremely simple and incredibly advanced. It can be terrifying in the cosmic awareness it creates, and yet, basically, it gives reassurance to the soul that it is never lost or abandoned, even if it appears to be. There is always a reason for everything, and, just as the Bible tells us that 'The very hairs on your head are all numbered' and 'He seeth the sparrow fall', so the teaching of reincarnation is that each soul, its own individual self, is making progress all the time, even if that progress has to involve moving temporarily backwards.

The details of exactly how the process of moving through a succession of lives takes place is also something that worries people:

'Do we choose our parents?'

'If we know we are going to die in a terrible accident, and we have been shown our life beforehand and accepted it, why can we not do something to stop the accident happening?'

'How many lives must we have?'

'What happens in the end, when the soul has learned everything?'

'Do we go straight into another life as soon as we die?'

'Could we live in two bodies at the same time—if one was a dying person, and the other was a baby born prematurely, for instance? I mean, the soul of the dying person might have been intended to go into the baby when it was born, only it came too soon.'

'Wouldn't this mean there was no heaven and hell—and what about Purgatory?'

Just as much of the hype surrounding

regressions can be hypnobabble—there is a certain off-handedness about regressing people these days, and people need no qualifications to be free to make claims that they can do this—so there can be no complete Guide to Reincarnation, with answers to every question, particularly in a book like this. I may feel I am able to give my own personal answers to some of the basic questions, out of my experience as a psychic and mystic and from what I have observed in the many past-life sessions I have conducted and experienced (as well as evidence from other sources). But no one on Earth can provide solid, cast-iron answers to questions concerning premature birth, or whether people who have been brain-dead for years can pass on into other bodies. Such splitting of hairs does not in any event really matter. The cases reported in these pages must speak for themselves.

Important basics which I do feel I can impart to sitters always give strength, positivity and reassurance:

The soul does not change, and, whether one comes back as a man or a woman (or even as an animal or creature from another planet, or something which has no sex as we know it), the essential spark of divine fire that we call the soul remains the same from beginning to end. One can never lose touch with one's own self, one's own identity.

Equally, no one will ever fail to recognize the souls of those they love—though there are different sorts and states of loving.

We possess free will at the same time as the choices we make are already known. No effort we ever make is lost, though we may not have been able to see the ground we have gained at that period in time. Nothing is without purpose, though we may not be able to recognize what that purpose is.

The Question of Time

The question of time is of vital relevance when dealing with the subject of reincarnation. On first approaching it, the average person automatically assumes that 'past lives' are in the past, and that the number of lives each soul may experience will occur in chronological order. It is sometimes difficult to envisage time as merely a human concept, something that is not there once the soul leaves the human condition. Yet this is in fact so.

When linking in to past lives I find, as I have mentioned previously, that they do generally make themselves known in some kind of sequence, usually working backwards, so that the Victorian era gives place to the Elizabethan, then to Roman or ancient Babylonian, and back to prehistory. However, there is another consideration that seems to override chronology, and that is the relevance and importance of each life. The existence that has the most relevance to the present situation will come through first, especially if its message is particularly urgent.

We all know that time is relative, even in this life—that it seems to stand still (when something very tragic occurs, for instance, and things happen 'in slow motion', or when we are experiencing great spiritual upliftment or physical ecstasy). Looking back over the years, time seems to be rather patchy; small incidents are remembered in vivid detail, and things we know we should recollect have been completely forgotten. In this way, time can appear very elastic—and it usually chooses what it will or won't make important in our memory, independently of our own volition. In the same way, souls that have become traumatized in the past and cannot pass easily in the way they are to go, do not just decide to stop and remain where they are. They have no control over such 'freezing' or 'stopping' of time, and they may need help to free themselves.

A brief moment in a past life can seem more vivid than what happened yesterday. The intensity of the experience has nothing to do with chronology or the period in history when it took place. People who have experienced regression, or even linking-in via someone like myself, can feel as though the life they knew in the past is just as real as the present— sometimes more so.

There are various ways of accounting for the nature of time, and the most difficult thing about it is not understanding the explanations but letting go of our preconceived notion of linear, chronological time. As human beings, we begin our lives at birth. We progress week by week, month by month and year by year, moving forward all the time. We grow older, and eventually die. Even the idea that the soul is later born again in a new body seems to imply that the chronology continues: that time moves forwards and can never stop, or go back, or jump about.

But if we remember that the soul lives separately from its human shell, and if we consider the way our minds deal with time, we can see that, to the mind, time has no chronological barriers. We can look forward; we can return to events that happened a long time ago in our childhood; we can dwell consciously in the present and hold on to the moment. We cannot, obviously, take our human bodies with us in and out of time—but the soul *can* move in this way, and (according to one theory) the events that have happened, or are happening or are going to happen, may occur in a circle: always returning to the beginning, so that there is no beginning and no end. Or else everything, past, present and future, could well be happening simultaneously, so that when we link in to a 'past life' it is actually as much of a real,

92

ongoing present as the life we are experiencing now. The main conclusion to be drawn from all these different theories is that 'past lives' do not fade away as time passes or become 'old'; when we link in with them we find they can be as real and as relevant to us as the present *now*.

Bardo

More subtle than the question of how many lives each individual may pass through is the question of what happens in between them. Does the soul leap, as it were, from the grave to the cradle, or is there a period of time allowed before the next incarnation?

In my experience both can happen at various times, though how the details are decided is something it is impossible to speak of with any real authority. This is extra-complex, because outside the human condition time, as we are aware of it, does not exist—so words like 'year' and 'month' are not applicable, although human beings undergoing regression do use them. Some authorities would dispute this, but my own experiences of past lives have been largely outside time, so that prehistoric lives might have been happening in a sort of vacuum alongside every other era—ancient Egyptian, Roman, Medieval and Victorian, as well as those which carried no date.

I also came to believe, after some time working with and studying past lives, that this 'momentary consciousness' and awareness only of the *now* is part of the reason why I personally get very few details along the lines of precise names, including place names ... and dates. Such things only block the soul's awareness of experiencing human living—apart from the fact that in a great many cases, as I have mentioned earlier, the people concerned would not have been able to tell me the year (10 million BC?) or the place (a rain forest, or a cave?).

But what does happen to the soul between lives? All the great religions that give instruction of reincarnation have something to say on the matter. The most comprehensive information can be found in the manuscript known as the *Tibetan Book of the Dead*.

In some places, Tibet included, the dead body is ceremonially carried to some high place by those known as 'the body-breakers', and, under the watchful and expectant gaze of hungry vultures, it is deliberately broken in pieces, dismembered and left for the vultures to deal with. Even the bones are ground down into powder and disposed of. The destruction of the body is complete. The letting go of the physical body after death, to whatever degree, is a necessity recognized intuitively by all living souls, whatever their beliefs. Only then can the spirit pass on. And where does it pass to? Where does it go?

Traditionally, prayers are repeated by holy

94

men for forty-nine days (seven times the magical number seven), while the spirit, now dead and physically removed from its earthly body, begins its wandering between lives—a state known as *bardo*. This complicated state, where the spirit will see visions, is comprehensively described in the *Tibetan Book of the Dead* (*Bardo Thodrol*).

It appears that the visions that the soul can experience dictate what will happen to it. These visions, which may be horrific, can terrify the soul and cause it to return hastily in a new body; alternatively, if it has the wisdom to recognize that the horrors are merely illusion, it will be able to pass on and be freed from the cycle of eternal rebirth. In most cases the soul is unable to achieve the necessary wisdom, and so must continue the process of learning all over again.

Speculation and theory are all very well, but I personally feel satisfied only if I have experienced at least something at first hand and can go on from there. In the case of *bardo*, working alone, and without any knowledge at the time of what I had done, I encountered regression to visions of both the extremes of horror and spiritual wisdom. As in all cases of psychic and mystic activity, I found that the vision is a personal thing, individual to each spirit. There are no 'mass-produced' horrors or glories in the worlds beyond this one: each is the soul's own, dictated by its needs and its fears.

Later, working with Gerry M., a fellow psychic I had known for several years, I obtained some interesting and fascinating corroborative material on the *bardo*—again without any particular effort in this direction. Gerry's case contained a great deal of other evidence of immense value. I detail it below, and my comments.

The Case of Gerry M.

In her early forties, Gerry was stunningly blonde, slim, something of a loner by nature, and had an awareness as complex and detailed as Angie's about her spiritual origins. She, too, had experienced alien encounters, and she told me that, as a young child, she had seen very tall, fair beings of light moving up and down the stairs of her home.

'I could almost see through them, so I used to call them the polythene people,' she revealed. 'They terrified me.'

Such consciousness often goes hand in hand with great psychic ability, and Gerry was exceptionally clairvoyant. Apart from her experiences with the aliens, however, we had never discussed past lives in any detail until the first time I sat down to do a 'past-life session' with her.

I linked in to the first life, and was able to describe it quite comprehensively.

'You were a young child—a girl, aged about six—and you seem to have lived somewhere northerly, among ice and mountains. I seem to get glaciers or ice, rather than snow, though. A village—of little wooden huts, it seems like— and you are holding onto your father's coat (a short sort of jacket) with your hand, following him through the houses. There was some great disaster happening, not a landslide, not a flood exactly, but something that not only wiped out the village where you lived, but destroyed the whole valley.'

She waited, and I added:

'You seem to have been handicapped in some way—I think you were dumb, perhaps deaf as well. But you were aware of what was happening, and knew that you had to die in the disaster. Your life was short, but it was very important that you should have just *been there* at that time, almost as if your presence was necessary, but why I can't tell you.'

I asked Gerry whether she could relate this episode to her present life, and she nodded.

'Yes ... Do you think the disaster might have been a tidal wave?'

'It could have been,' I said, considering. 'I see ice and mountains, and you are wearing a pointed hood ... your father wearing skins, furs. But it was not an avalanche, not a landslide, nor a flood, though it was something that poured into the valley. A tidal wave is probably the nearest thing, at a guess, though I have never heard of tidal waves in the northern hemisphere. They knew it was coming, everyone was thronging together, trying to escape.'

'I dream of tidal waves and drowning, very often,' she told me. 'I have dreamed of them all my life. And I was very close to my father as a child. I can identify with that, the feeling I would have followed him and held on to his coat.'

'You do not seem to have had a mother,' I said.

'No, I have never felt that I was close to my mother in this life,' she admitted.

I pointed out that the child had been small and unable to express herself, that she had relied on the grip she had upon her father's jacket, and that she would have felt lost, abandoned and alone when the disaster struck and she was parted from him.

'You needed him, he was your foundation, your security. You felt as though you could not manage without him.'

She agreed that in the present, she had found it extremely hard to assert her own identity and was still struggling to be able to live and manage independently, free of the almost panic-stricken love/hate need she felt for others—generally not as able as herself—to control her.

'When do you think this life happened?' she asked. I thought it had been towards the end of the last century; it seemed to be close, and to foreshadow her struggles in this life. Also it had been very brief, and seemed to have been a sort of preparation, or even rehearsal, for her more detailed spiritual and emotional journeys in her present existence.

The second life I linked into was so painful that I felt myself picking up the deep hurts as though I was raw and bleeding myself, and could hardly speak for the knot of tears in my throat. My eyes stung.

'You were not able to express yourself then, either,' I said. 'You were a female gorilla or some type of large monkey . . . dark coarse fur. It was medieval Europe—Spain, I think—and I see you in a tall, barred cage on wheels, just existing. The cage was only a few feet square; you were unable to move and, though I don't think you were beaten or goaded or starved, you were alone, alien, exposed—rotting really. It was no life at all, just a slow death. You were aware, and your suffering was very great. You just endured. You have suffered a great deal in the past—perhaps more than you needed to.'

Gerry revealed that: 'I have never been able to go to zoos or circuses, and it was a family joke that no one could take me near any caged or performing animals as a child. I would embarrass everyone by screaming frantically until I was taken away. I can identify very strongly with the gorilla and feel for her.'

'It appears that in past lives you had some

part to play which involved carrying suffering,' I said.

'Does that mean I committed some awful crime?' she enquired. 'That I have had to pay for it?'

But, this time, I thought not.

'Your connection with the alien beings, your deep awareness of other life forms, would suggest that you were sent here, perhaps to carry suffering that would be too great for other, weaker souls. The little girl had to be there when the disaster, whatever it was, came; I don't know why or what for, except that by being there, she achieved something. I feel as though your personal struggles and emotional difficulties—with relating to others and being unable to assert yourself as a person in your own right—are separate from the task you are here to carry out. And I do feel your sufferings have been extreme, but that often you have chosen the suffering when you did not need to. Do you see what I mean?'

She nodded slowly.

'So I'm a masochist?'

'Perhaps. Certainly you identify with the victim, and generally victims choose their role to some degree. Some people find it difficult to let go of their suffering, because they have never known anything else, and they are frightened at the thought of things actually going right for a change. It is hard to move beyond the boundaries one has always known, and freedom can actually be extremely hard to cope with.'

'Yes.' Her nod was decisive now. 'I have been trying to break away. . . . It is tough, and it is frightening, and I am inclined to get drawn into situations with people which are very similar to those I have known.'

'That is always the way,' I agreed. 'The patterns repeat themselves. For as long as you regard yourself mentally as a victim, a loser, then you will be attracted to people who treat you that way. I do feel, though, that the past lives were of far more significance than just patterns of low self-esteem. But what that significance was will have to remain a mystery. You are very spiritual, very elevated, you are open to other life forms and have close experience of alien activity. Let's try a third life.'

When I linked in I told her that I saw first of all an empty space of sand, like a very burned desert, which stretched to the horizon. There did not seem to be any landmark at all, only the sand and a wide sky above. I felt the time was primitive, or perhaps not even real as we know reality, since the scene was so empty.

'You have come from some other place, and I see you as an egg, just there on the sand,' I told her. 'The egg means that you can hatch out of it to become anything you like—you can choose your own body and shape, your own existence. There are no creatures around at all, but I see the possibility of an ostrich attracts you—and I get the feeling this place might have been somewhere in Australia, before it was populated at all. I see the possibility of an ostrich, now the possibility of a crocodile or lizard, hatching in a river—something to do with rocky waters, at any rate.'

'Where did the egg come from?' Gerry enquired.

'Well, it seems to have come from some other place. Maybe outside of the Earth. I think you were sent, and with a purpose, but you came in this form and were allowed to choose the life you would lead. I cannot see what you decided to become, and I don't know what the purpose was, nor who—or what—sent you. It may have something to do with the suffering you have undergone.'

We finished the sitting on that interesting note, and some months later, when Gerry was still struggling with her attempts to establish herself as an independent personality and following the path of her spiritual journey, we met again to conduct a regression session.

Regression Session: Gerry M., 27 February 1966

Gerry was lying comfortably, covered with a light, warm shawl. I began by relaxing her and directing her to go back to a time and place in this life where she had been very happy. She described the top of a mountain in Israel, a

102

place where she had spent some time and which she often talked about as the source of her spiritual inspiration. I asked her to move further back in her present life.

G.: I can see a Roman soldier.
D.: Tell me more about him.
G.: I dunno. I can just see his ... sort of ... armoured skirt [*long pause*].
D.: Where was this?
G.: I don't really know. I think I'm still in the Middle East somewhere.
D.: Let him go, just let him drift away. Breathe deeply, slowly; relax.
[I directed her to a time before she had been born.]
G.: [*long pause*] I was at sea, on a boat. Boat's going up and down, up and down—a sailing ship.
D.: What sea was it?
G.: [*half-laugh*] A rough one. Might have been the English Channel ... [*after long pause, suddenly*) I was a man—-I think I might have been a similar age to the age I am now [*early 40s*] but more lived in, more experienced, sort of.
D.: Can you tell me your name?
G.: [*without hesitation*] Elliot.
D.: What were you feeling at that time?
G.: Just loved the sea. Looking out at the horizon, on the move, loved the movement.
D.: Are you alone?

G.: Part of a crew.

D.: What type of ship?

G.: Sailing ship—wooden planks and deck, you know ... A very even-tempered person, pleasurable, very balanced; on the move all the time, never got sick.

[I asked what Elliot remembered when he thought back to wherever his home had been.]

G.: His mother—and a house, a little terrace house.

D.: What does he think of his mother?

G.: Someone stable, always there, secure, the same as him, happy to see him. Even-tempered, the same, motherly, solid.

D.: Do you feel more at home with Elliot than with Gerry?

G.: I should say ... Yeah, everything was so simple. On the move all the time—the horizon was always there in front of him. Life was one adventure after another, and still with somewhere to go home to.

D.: Was he never unhappy?

G.: When he got cold—he hated the cold, the damp.

D.: Did he used to sing?

G.: Yes, all the time—I sing all the time.

D.: What did he sing? Can you sing it to me?

G.: [*after a moment*] He sang laments ... um ... um ... a bit Irish, actually.

D.: Don't try to analyse it, just tell me what he sang.

G.: ... Quite sad songs.

D.: Does that mean he was sad?

G.: Yeah, you . . . he didn't know it, though . . . yeah, you're right in a way.

D.: I am asking you: if he sang sad songs, laments, doesn't that indicate he might have felt unhappy?

G.: Singing those very heartfelt songs. . . . No. I don't feel unhappy, I feel . . . um . . . sort of wistful and hopeful—that sort of thing—much more than pessimistic or sad . . . His temperament wasn't like that at all.

D.: Did he like everybody round him—the crew?

G.: [*promptly*] No, some he couldn't stand. Some of the guys he couldn't stand. They were like beasts.

D.: What is the year?

G.: The year is Seventeen Forty- . . . five.

D.: What nationality was he?

G.: . . . Stripes and that—my first reaction was to say Dutch, with pale blue-and-white striped trousers.

D.: What was his position on the ship?

G.: Middle. Wasn't high or low. Good worker, but not given important jobs to do. One of the things he used a lot was his strength . . . muscles.

D.: . . . I suppose they all did. What country did his mother live in, do you know?

G.: [*short pause*] Ireland.

D.: Did he have a wife? A sweetheart?

G.: He met someone on a journey once—

someone he fell in love with. And this is both the hope and the return—of her, of falling in love like that, and hoping to return.

D.: Why did he not do something about it at the time?

G.: Boat was leaving. It was his limit. His limit was up; it was coming to an end.

D.: Where did this take place?

G.: . . . A very busy port. South America.

D.: What nationality was she?

G.: Looks Spanish.

[Gerry was questioned about Elliot's appearance and feelings.]

G.: Blond hair, lot of it, blue eyes—maybe that's his Dutch origins . . . Tallish. He was very secure with himself, very even-keeled. The señorita type he dreamed about symbolized the ultimate.

D.: What happened to him at the end of his life?

G.: [*very long pause*] I think he died on the boat—heart attack. He just crumpled.

[I talked Gerry through into a subsequent life. She said she had been a little girl.]

D.: Where did your soul go after you were Elliot?

G.: . . . Somewhere very very high.

D.: What was it doing?

G.: [*soft, broken phrases*] Gaining energy in some sense.

D.: Tell me about the little girl.

G.: Sort of Victorian type, I suppose. Just a

little girl.

D.: Does she look rich? Poor?

G.: Rich—well, clean. She looks clean.

D.: How old is she?

G.: About eight.

D.: What is she doing?

G.: Dancing innocently ... Watching something. She's watching a carnival—animals ... No, it's not ... actually, she's looking at a poster—looks like it's of a bear, juggling balls.

D.: Where is the poster?

G.: On a wall. She's looking at the bear ... There's a lot of red all along the bottom ... I don't think she's sure about reading.

D.: Can you tell me her name?

G.: [*doubtfully*] Begins with an M. Mirabelle ... Mirabella ... something like that. She's fascinated by this bear juggling with these balls.

D.: Does she want to see the bear?

G.: Oh, yeah. She's never seen animals before, only toys.

D.: How did that happen? [*Had she missed seeing horses, dogs, cats?*]

G.: I think it's 'cos it's a bear—wild, and big.

[Gerry was instructed to go forward in time until the girl was 16, and asked what she was doing.]

G.: She's gone really slim and tall, and she's wearing a hat.

D.: What sort of hat?

G.: A strange-looking bonnet, complicated—sort of ... tilts up in front.

D.: What else is she wearing?

G.: A cloak—a most beautiful powder blue.

D.: How do you feel about her? Do you like her?

G.: Not particularly, no.

[Gerry was instructed to go forward to when the girl was 25]

D.: Now what is she doing?

G.: She's so puritanical. Pious, and 'us-and-them' type, so judgemental. God-fearing. All Lut . . . Lus . . . Lutheran.

D.: How did this happen?

G.: I think it had to do with her family—small privileges. Like the beast on the poster . . . she can't work out why she's been lucky, except that, you know, some have and others don't have, and the ones who have must be better. And, yes, she just *knows* she's better than everyone else.

D.: Was anyone responsible for making her think so?

G.: Her father—and her mother.

D.: Did she have brothers and sisters?

G.: No.

[Gerry was instructed to move on to when the girl was 45.]

G.: [*startled*] She's in black. [*long pause*]

D.: What sort of clothes is she wearing?

G.: A long black mourning dress. I think it's for her parents—her father.

D.: Does she have a husband?

G.: [*impatiently*] No, nothing like that. But I

think she's beginning to feel a bit. Her authoritarian father kept her so rigid all the time ... but she's starting to feel more alive.
D.: How does she feel about that?
G.: Uncomfortable ... shocked about it really.
[Gerry was instructed to move on to when the girl was 65.]
D.: She's much happier, quite fat, laughs now. I think she sort of went back to the joy of looking at the poster—life turned into an adventure again.
D.: What caused this?
G.: ... She met someone, another woman, and made friends with her. And even if she was just ... like, on the staff of her house, this woman opened up her eyes to living, and made her realize that there were nice people around—instead of her thinking everyone was all the same.
[Gerry was talked through to a previous life of her own choosing. She could not identify the date, but said the life was 'One that matters to me' and that the number 13 was connected with it.]
G.: [*after a long, long pause and some gentle prompting*] Weird. This is not a normal thing ... not even a landscape.
D.: What do you feel?
G.: A sort of excitement. It's really weird; it's like looking at the end of the Earth in outer space, like a planet. It's like looking over the curvature of the Earth.

D.: What sort of perspective do you have? . . .
Who are you?

G.: . . . Don't know. I can't tell. Not human as
we know it.

D.: What are you doing?

G.: . . . Don't quite know—if I'm . . . I can't get
the image of a spider out of my mind. I don't
know if it's because my limbs are very long, or
if I *am* a spider.

D.: What can you see? . . . You said you were
looking at the curvature of the Earth.

G.: Everything seems huge. But I suppose it
would seem huge if I was tiny.

D.: Can you think? Or just feel?

G.: . . . No, it's more instinct, quite honestly . . .

D.: Do you feel anything at all?

G.: Tell you what, noises are really strong,
noises are like crashes all around.

D.: Can you move your legs?

G.: Yeah, 'swhat I mean. I've got all these legs.

D.: What do they feel like?

G.: They're sensitive—very, very sensitive.
They've got hairs on them . . . they're very,
very, very much more sensitive than our legs.
They're delicate . . . delicate, and I know . . .
that my main instinct is . . . be careful of my
legs.

D.: Are you happy?

G.: There's just nothing. Nothing like that.

D.: Are you afraid?

G.: Yeah, very.

D.: What are you doing?

110

G.: Walking very slowly—all these legs moving in unison.

D.: Is there anything else around you that you can tell me about? [*long pause*] Any colours?

G.: Everything is . . . like, black and white . . . like all black, shades of dark. Maybe no colour in my vision.

D.: What do you feel when you move your legs?

G.: There's such a crashing, the leaves and things under me are so loud—and every leg that goes down is so delicate.

D.: Is there anything around to alarm you?

G.: Everything. Every movement . . . every shadow, every shadow is a threat. When I said I don't feel, it was . . . like, not positive . . . living more in a state totally threatened by every shadow.

D.: Are you on your own?

G.: I am. But there's others, littler than me— I'm quite big actually. They're the same, but littler.

D.: What are they doing?

G.: Scurrying. They're behind me, to the right. Teeming.

[Gerry was directed to take the soul back before it had entered the spider and asked what it was doing.]

G.: Something very powerful. I just feel this power—energize is too weak a word . . . sort of reinforced.

D.: Where are you?

G.: Where? A place like an . . . [*long pause*] A

shelf . . . like being shelved . . . nothing much happening.

D.: What can you see?

G.: Like a bookcase shelf, sort of.

D.: Are you alone?

G.: Yeah, very much so.

D.: How do you feel?

G.: Resting, depleted.

D.: You mentioned the power, the energy.

G.: That's where it came from—getting energized.

D.: Can you tell me what you look like?

G.: On the shelf . . . I've got the image of a sort of oval.

D.: What colour?

G.: Well . . . lighter than the shelf.

D.: What is it made of?

G.: . . . Well, it's not dissimilar to a slightly long egg.

D.: Are there any others?

G.: Thousands of them, all lying there—nobody about, just these shelves.

[Gerry was recalled safely from her trance.]

From my Notes on Gerry M.'s Two Sessions

1. Interesting that she obviously suffered in animal form, but did not react in the same way to the introduction of performing animals in another context. She is also, among other things, a qualified cook, (though mainly a vegetarian cook) and handles raw meat. Has a

112

maturity of spirit brought a sense of perspective, a more rational approach to the subject of suffering animals?

2. My feeling was that the first two 'lives' in her regression were extensions of her personality in this life.

3. Both sessions independently reached the image of the egg, and her description of the egg 'resting' between lives (in the *bardo* state?) fits in with my sensation that the egg had been delivered into the world ready to be born. All life comes from some sort of egg (*ovum*) and she might just as well have hatched out into a spider as an ostrich or crocodile. I had no means of assessing the size of the egg I saw.

4. Follow-up research in the local library revealed the information that spiders—or, at least, most types of spiders—possess short-sighted eyes that see clearly for only a very short distance and detect blurred shadows and light/dark beyond. Also, spiders have ear 'hairs' on their legs, which they rely on for information more than their eyes. The Invertebrate Department at the Royal Zoological Society in Regent's Park verified this and added that, because of their shortness of sight, spiders would be far more likely to notice a moving shadow in the vicinity than a shape or colour.

Gerry has never studied biology or entomology, and has no reason to have investigated the characteristics of spiders in

113

order to produce this very accurate—but restricted—'life'. It seemed to cause her genuine amazement and incredulous fascination as she described it to me.

5. My impressions were that Gerry has, over a great many lifetimes, become able to move through different realities and planes of existence without effort, and that she has often—as in the case of the little girl in the disaster—provided a token presence, so that she can represent spirits that cannot speak for themselves. In that case it was the dead and the lost (she is a qualified medium). Other lives (the spider and the gorilla) indicate other life forms: and her alien experiences reveal a very wide awareness into which she can link almost at will.

CHAPTER SIX

HAVE WE MET BEFORE?

Vivien, a 49-year-old writer, independent, successful, just recovering from a broken marriage, walked into the basement hall of her local Spiritualist Church intending to join a group of acquaintances for tea and biscuits after the service.

'There was a figure of a man sitting on his own,' she recalls. 'Very quiet, a bit lonely, I suppose, but I didn't even see his face, I didn't notice. I just knew I had to go to him, so I held out my hand and laughed and said something—you know, "Have we met?" or something like that—and he took my hand and held it and said "No, we haven't." I said "I thought you were the actor from last week," and he said "No, I'm not an actor, but I do astrology, and if you would like your horoscope done, and a cup of tea, I live only a few streets away".'

She adds simply, without embarrassment, 'So of course, I went.'

The memories, recollections and regressions that have materialized since Vivien's meeting with Liam have underscored a link between their souls that is centuries old. Four years later, they are still, somewhat stormily, together, and, although occasionally they find the other difficult to live with, each is the lodestone to which the other's soul is drawn, seemingly by fate and destiny—by the workings of karma (something subtly different from human commitment and love).

'I knew from the start that I had to support Liam and give him the encouragement and belief he needed. I just knew I had to be with him and for him one hundred and ten per cent, no questions asked. I didn't understand why or how, and reason didn't come into it.'

'When did the awareness of your joint past lives begin?' I ask Vivien, and she laughs mischievously.

'Well, we both knew right from the first moment, although nothing was said. And we are both psychic, so there were some, well, unusual closenesses of thought which are difficult to explain. But after about six months with Liam, I developed chronic back pain which almost crippled me. I tried all sorts of treatment, from spiritual healing to acupuncture to visiting an osteopath, but nothing seemed to do any good. And then I heard that back pain doesn't really exist, it is caused by blocks in energy from this life or from the past, so I started to concentrate on this idea with relation to my back problem.'

'And did the pain go away?'

'No, it didn't actually, but one day I saw, as clearly as though I was watching a film, a past life where I had been some sort of English yeoman at the time of the Crusades. I saw a battle taking place under a burning sun, everywhere very hot and dusty, rock and sand. And as I turned—I was a big, burly man, more muscle than brain—an arrow came from the side and went deep into my left hip, towards the back, exactly in the place where the source of the pain seems to be. I could see myself fall, the way everything sort of suddenly became different—as though the whole focus of my existence altered—and I knew I was dying. Blurring and blackness.

'Well, as I say, this vision didn't do anything to help my back pain, and I thought that was

116

odd, because if you can identify the cause of something you are carrying from the past—the original cause of the trouble—the common theory is that the symptoms will then just disappear. Anyway, I continued to meditate on that scene, the battle and the injury, and I saw something else emerge after a while. I had not died in the battle, I had lain there on the sand in, I think, a sort of feverish trance, and when it was evening—a mixture of night coming on and lights, flames—someone came to me and stood looking down at me. He had a lean, dark face and piercing eyes and he was wearing some sort of dark robe. He had been a Saracen or Moorish physician and he had me taken to his house and removed the arrow and saved my life. And I know that man was Liam.'

'Really?'

'Yes, I even asked Liam about it and he remembers his past life as that Moorish doctor-scholar. But there was another occasion when he saved my life, as well. I thought a lot about possible links between us, especially in view of the way we seemed to have been brought together. Other people told me it was fate and destiny, and one very psychic woman looked at Liam's picture and said he had a heavy karma to carry. She said to me: "Don't try to carry it for him. He can carry it, but it would kill you."

'Anyway, in the process of meditating this other vision just came to me, a little while after the scene with the arrow. I had a vivid picture

117

of myself in some time and place that must have been an early Mediterranean sort of civilization, or perhaps Atlantis. I was not a human being. I don't know what I was, some sort of tiny elemental spirit, like a little silver creature, and I could fly, but I had no wings.'

'A type of ancient Tinkerbell?' I ask, smiling.

'Well, yes in a way, even though that sounds rather dreadful. But, you know, I think that the things that turn up as clichés in imaginative and science fiction are often actually based on realities that we carry with us from folk memory and ancient awareness we can't explain. This little silver entity might well have been some sort of "faery" but it had no wings, no gauzy dress, nothing like that. I was trapped, as this little entity, inside a large earthenware jar—the sort that grain, or wine, is stored in in the East—and there was a lid of sorts over the top, so that it was dark.

'My first thought when the memory came through was that I had been a bird, or a butterfly, and I was sort of hovering there in the dark, lost and unable to escape. But the fact that I had no wings at all rubbed out the idea of a bird or insect. I was just energy, I did not need wings. Later, the picture clarified itself, as they do. The jar was standing in a room about half-way up a tower, in some sort of building that was white stone, with sunshine outside and the sea below. The room was a sort of workroom or laboratory belonging to a high priest/magus/wise-man-type of person of great knowledge and power. There were other things trapped there, entities and specimens in bottles—and I knew that the great man had become obsessed with knowledge for its own sake and was meddling in matters of life and death. In a similar way,' she adds pointedly, 'to what scientists are doing now.'

'I felt he had turned away from the spiritual source of his power, and had become "dark" because of his obsession. But then I was aware of someone taking away the lid of the jar, and I looked up into a dark face looming above me. I was allowed to go, and I can remember shooting at an incredible speed out of the depths of the jar, straight for a small window behind the man's head, set in the wall. It had no glass, and I shot straight out and up into a sky that was the most glorious sunlit blue. I do not remember anything after that, but I know that the magician was Liam, and that he freed me when I was trapped and dying.'

'What does he say about this?' I query.

Vivien is very thoughtful.

'He can remember Atlantis, or wherever the place was, better than I can. He has had other lives—I have worked with him on regressions myself—and some of them are very notable, but these two, where our lives touched so dramatically, make a great deal of sense with regard to our lives today. He saved me on at least two occasions, and it is as though I am

119

impelled by something outside myself to do all I can to "save" him in return in this life. Not his life—that is not really in danger—but his soul, or even, maybe, his sanity.'

'Isn't that being rather melodramatic?'

'No,' she says seriously. 'He is a man of great spiritual gifts and power, but that "dark" side is still there, a sort of spiritual pride and arrogance that gets in the way of true spiritual development—the heavy karma, I suppose, that is hard to carry and can crush the soul.'

'How do you think you are helping him?'

'Just by being there,' Vivien answers simply. 'It is not up to me to decide—or even to know—how I can best help. But there does seem to be a very strong karmic link, and I feel as though there is some debt for me to clear, which I don't understand but which, in return for my life in previous existences, I owe to Liam.

'I just try to do what I can. He has deep emotional problems as well and, being the powerful character he is, he doesn't find it easy to listen to doctors or psychiatrists. But I have recently started working with him using a method called Transactional Analysis, so hopefully it might make a difference to his peace of mind.'

'You think you will be able to cure him in the end?' I query.

'I don't think karmic debts work like that,' Vivien says after a moment. 'I don't know whether there will be any end at all. Or any cure, as such. Maybe we will have to spend other lifetimes together, giving each other support; he has saved me, I am trying to help him—perhaps it is all the same thing, really.'

When interviewed separately, Liam added the following observations on what Vivien had said, speaking partly in a self-induced regressive trance state:

Regarding the battle scene and the arrow wound:

'I was called Baba al Rashid. It means Master, or Chief, and something like "The trembling of the wind in the branches."

'I saw her lying down with a swelling in her arm where she had tripped and had a multiple-chip fracture of her arm, and I treated the arm with herbs and balm, then when she was soothed, I proceeded to remove the arrow from her hip and treat the wound. While I was treating her, she made strange noises in the night, a bit like a miniature bear eating eucalyptus leaves, which I once heard singing in a gum tree.'

'Why did you choose to save her? There must have been many other people who were wounded.'

'The colours of her dress seemed to blend well, yet contrast with the desert. She seemed to stand out.'

'Did you then see her as a woman?'

'The colours moved, making an angelic form

round the man, and I thought at first it might be dead because of this vision, not for any medical reason.'

Regarding the scene in the priest-scientist's room:

'In Atlantis my priest name was Mavahantis.

'I was placing a bigger jar on the shelf containing a pygmy tribal chief when the sunlight reflected off another jar standing on the table—it was metal with a cork and wax cap, very intricate, made of resin with glass filigree round the edges. There was a sort of window in the bottle, like a ship's porthole, made of fused light-blue glass. As I looked into this it was like an eye winking at me. I stared into the glass, holding the jar with my right hand; my left hand trembled, releasing the stopper as if by act of God. A glowing spark shot by my shoulder—like a dewdrop, upside down.'

'Did you recognise Vivien?'

'As the spark shot up there seemed to be a sort of misty incense veil falling down. As I looked into this I recognized a woman I had loved from afar. I thought this person was lost and gone, but found that she had returned— and felt that she would return again.'

Regarding their meeting in this life:

'It's a funny thing, in this life when I met this woman again, although in a public place, I was very tired and in a haze, and we went to discuss the karma of astrology, entering a dim room in

122

my house, lit by a flickering, faint computer screen. In this twilight world, I recognized her by her auric inner light, which outshone her faint, shadowy, bodily form.'

'How do you feel about your destiny of saving or helping each other?'

'This was the start of a more difficult phase of an already difficult life and somehow she inspired me to work through the difficulties.'

*   *   *

The sense of having known someone in a previous existence is not the joke some people would believe. In romantic fiction villainous types have rolled their eyes and declared (untruthfully), 'I remember wandering with you on the banks of the Tigris in the moonlight, with night-flowering blossoms scenting the air,' as they attempt to seduce the heroine. This is psychologically good sense, for nothing can lower the defences more than the feeling that one shares a common memory reaching back as far as one can recall. The other person who has been there has become, through shared experience, almost a part of oneself, and— especially if the way has been long, difficult and often blurred and lost in the past—the presence of another who has shared it is immensely reassuring, even if that other was not always loved. Bonds of hate can be just as powerful.

Meeting someone and bypassing all the elements of 'getting to know' them, because recognition is in some way instantaneous, is another phenomenon that is joked about, but it does happen, and is usually ascribed to fate, destiny, kismet or karma. There have even been cases where souls (up to large numbers) have claimed to reincarnate in groups—though more commonly they will meet up in pairs, as in the case of Vivien and Liam.

* * *

Jill and Sandor were a generation apart. He had, in the popular idiom, already lived a life of action and had a wife and grown-up children. She had not yet completed studying for her degree. When they had met it was, they explained, as though everything else—time, place, age, the other people in their lives—simply faded away. They each recognized instinctively that only the other was real, that everything else was illusion.

'We knew we had to cope in the real world,' Sandor said, with a wry smile. 'There was no hurry, no dramatic changes of plan, no throwing up jobs and families. We didn't need to do that, it was as though we knew there was all the time in the world—or out of it—and, so long as the other was there, we were just getting through what we had done many times before. I am quite certain I recognized Jill the

124

moment I set eyes on her, and she says she knew me.'

Jill nodded, and I asked:

'Could you explain how?'

They exchanged glances, then Sandor shrugged.

'Difficult to say. To me it was as though I'd been marking time, waiting for her without realizing it; and then, when I saw her, I could let the mask fall—all my life so far with it—and become real.'

'It does have something to do with a reality that has no connection with ordinary existence,' Jill added. 'As though you suddenly step into another dimension, and you two are the only ones there.'

'Not just love at first sight? Across a crowded room and all that?'

They seemed puzzled.

'No, not at all, really.' Jill spoke for both. 'The love was there long before I saw Sandor. I was just put in touch with it again. This type of thing isn't really love as people imagine it, though I won't deny I do love him in a sexual way too. But . . . well, if Romeo and Juliet had had this sort of love, they wouldn't have needed to die for it. They would have done all the dying in the early days, centuries ago, and come to see that dying doesn't really enter into it. It's a state of peacefulness, not passion. Somehow the other person strengthens your own identity, helps you to view yourself with clarity and definition.'

*　*　*

Maureen, wide-eyed and expectant, was thrilled to be having a past-life session because, she frankly admitted, she had never tried anything like it before and was very curious to see what might emerge. As I linked in to her past lives, I picked up several of a young and lovely girl—once in Victorian times, once as the daughter of a high-ranking Roman official 'in exile' serving in the north, probably somewhere in Roman Britain.

The girl, somewhat unusually, was identifiable in each case because she looked exactly the same. She also seemed to be doing nothing, just 'being there' in effect, in rather the same way that Gerry M. had lent a token presence in the situations in which she had appeared.

'I don't think,' I said to Maureen, 'that you have any problems, either without or within, which you cannot cope with.'

She pondered.

'No, I think I could cope.'

'And you don't seem to want anything particularly. You seem to be quite happy with things as they are.'

'Money, you mean?'

'No, everything. Relationships, dreams, the realizing of ambitions, fulfilling of hopes. You

126

seem so completely self-contained that there is something odd about it.'

Again she pondered, then smiled.

'Well, there are things that might be pleasant—but, no, I don't really need them.'

I had already established that Maureen had great psychic potential, though she had never developed her powers or begun to understand how they worked. Now I began to feel some sort of presence around her and asked:

'Do you think someone might be trying to get in touch with you? Someone who is dead? I can pick up a strong presence around.'

As we progressed, it seemed that the spirit which was making its presence felt might have been a grandmother ... an aunt. I could not make it out clearly, nor exactly why it was there.

'It's odd,' I told Maureen. 'I think there is a very strong spirit presence around you, and not just one person. I seem to see a sort of group, belonging together, and you are one of them. You are here from some very high plane, and your lives in the past were the same, more or less. Just being there, lending your presence.'

'Where have I come from? What sort of plane?' she asked.

'Well, no joking, but something angelic— and there is more than one of you—but I don't think you reincarnate all together, you take turns, and as one tires another will take over. In the meantime the rest give spiritual strength and energy. They are around you now, giving you support. Do you feel them?'

'I suppose . . . yes, there is a sort of sense of being part of a family, a group. Yes, I think I can take that,' she agreed.

'It is as though you are a power source, between you, or guardians, and you have to cover a long distance, taking turns—like people in a relay race. Each of you does a "stint", then rests while another takes over. You just have to be there, for some reason; it is the work your group has been assigned. And the others have always been there, and will be there in the future. That is something I can guarantee—you will never, ever, be on your own.'

* * *

There have been cases where groups of people have claimed they regularly reincarnate all together. I can remember reading, years ago, in a paperback I cannot now trace entitled *I Am Mary Shelley* (possibly *I Was Mary Shelley*), how an American woman identified the whole cast of characters from Mary Shelley's life among her present-day relatives, friends and acquaintances. Mary was no insignificant peasant girl but the author of *Frankenstein*, her husband the poet Shelley, her close friend the poet Byron. Not only did everyone involved apparently recall, either spontaneously or under hypnosis, the details of their literary lives

128

and the tangled love affairs that they had carried on with the other characters, but they also held regular meetings where they all 'tripped' into other eras, and wandered round together in places like Atlantis and ancient Egypt.

The much-respected legal figure Christmas Humphreys also believed that he and his friends had lived their lives together in the past. I heard him speak on one occasion about their existence together and identities in ancient Rome. Personally, however, I have not (yet) come across a case of such mass incarnation on the human level that I would accept without further investigation.

There are several reasons for this. The first is that it is all too easy for individuals to seek 'safety in numbers' and attempt to escape, to whatever degree, the inevitable loneliness of the soul by identifying themselves in some sort of group. The idea of groups of human beings who incarnate together time after time, so that they are always comfortably protected by familiarity and never have to struggle alone, is a happy thought: one which would bring great reassurance if it could be proved true. But, since in my experience nothing (not even past existence) happens without a reason and in order to allow spiritual growth—which is often painful, and must inevitably take place alone— there seems to be no point in group reincarnations where the 'family' simply moves in and out of time.

What holds souls together are the threads of karmic energy, of paying off karmic debts, of settling 'unfinished business'. The workings out of karma, the cosmic law of cause and effect, of achieving balance and harmony, have little to do with human relationships on the level on which we know them. Some higher souls— those on angelic planes, for instance—may already have achieved the harmony and balance that 'new' souls, in their raw and painful state, are struggling to envisage. There seem to be many cases where the most unexpected (almost unlikely) spirits, are contributing simply by 'being here'. Others, even highly spiritual people, may still be locked in their karmic workings out, whether held by the positivity of love or the dark negativity of cruelty and hate.

*　*　*

During the course of Roberto's sitting it became obvious that in a past life he had been subjected to a terrifying physical attack, by an unknown assailant, and then left for dead. The small victim—a young child—was so traumatized that it was not aware it had died, and remained trapped in a permanent *now* of suffering. With Roberto's help, I freed it from its torment and we saw it safely on its way home, to the light where it belonged. But he confided that he thought the person who had used him so cruelly in the past was with him again in the present, once more following the pattern of cruelty and brutality.

'I see it differently now, though, after this,' he said. 'I can free myself now, I have the choice. But he—this other man—never can; not until he's paid for it all. That is a very terrible thing to wish on anybody.'

'You feel you don't hate him so much, then?'

'How can I hate him? I can get out this time. I'm not a small child, helpless. He cannot hurt me any more unless I let him. But he is hurting himself, piling up all this terrible karma—sin . . . whatever you call it—on his own head. I really feel . . .' His voice was very quiet. 'I never thought I would say this, but I really feel sorry for him.'

* * *

Vanda's case revealed many karmic threads which linked her soul to that of another. We began her past-life sitting.

'I have the most incredible sensation of water dripping very heavily,' I told her. 'But not straight down. It is coming through leaves, very tall trees and layers and layers of leaves, like thick green walls all around. Everywhere is the leaves; you cannot see the sky, if there is one. I think it is a rain forest, but where, or when, is impossible to tell.

131

'The water is underfoot, everywhere. Like tropical rain, I suppose, but it seems to have been going on for a very long time, as though it will never stop. You are trying to curl up and cower out of the rain, you are a child, some kind of native child, you are not wearing anything except maybe a bit of cloth around you, and you cannot walk. You are a cripple; you are also sick and thin, and you are alone. At least,' I added after a moment, 'you are alone, and yet you are not alone.'

Vanda's dark eyes were intent.

'I think there was a man,' I said slowly. 'There were just the two of you, the man and the small child. What you were doing there in the depths of the forest—with no shelter, no possessions, just cowering under the leaves—I have no idea. I think something must have happened like a plague, and he had hidden with you and tried to escape it. I don't know whether he was your father, or even whether there was a definite "father" role in that society. But you had to depend absolutely on him. You were close to starvation, ill, and he just left you and went. To get what? Food? Someone to nurse you? Or did he just go? I don't know what he went for, but he went, and you are lying there—sick, unable to move, the water dripping and running all around—just waiting for him to come back. You are not even old enough to be aware that you will die if he does not. Just waiting.'

132

When I asked Vanda whether she could relate this to her present life, she said after a moment:

'It's not obvious, because I wear long skirts and the right shoes, but I am crippled in this life too. The result of illness: polio as a child. And I completely accept the dependency on the man, because all my life, until my father died, I had a relationship with him that was exactly like that. I could never imagine life without him. I would panic at the thought of what would happen if he died. I seemed to exist only because he was there: far more than simply needing the support or the presence of a parent.'

'So you relied on him that much?'

'Yes, but the odd thing was that, though I was a child, he seemed to rely on me as well, to need some sort of strength I possessed. It was very strange and perhaps not altogether healthy.'

Vanda accepted my suggestion that she had brought both the state of complete dependency and the state of waiting with her from that early life—though it was difficult to say whether there had been any other lives in between. I felt that they would only have underlined the karmic bond of need between her soul and that of the man who had been her father in this life.

While we were talking, I began to sense the presence of someone who had died, who was attempting, increasingly urgently, to contact her, and I told her:

'I can see a man, he is on a road between buildings, near a post-box. There is a factory, or office with big windows on the other side of the road. Can you identify the place?'

'Yes,' Vanda said steadily. 'It is the last place I saw my father alive. I was working in one of the buildings, and I looked out of the window and saw him walk past along the street. He could not speak to me, of course, only look up at the windows, but he did lift his arm, as though he was waving.' She paused then added: 'He was dead a few hours later: a heart attack. So I never said goodbye to him—and he never said goodbye to me.'

'He has been unable to pass on, waiting to say that goodbye, to be able to let you go, and for you to let him go.' I told her.

Her voice was muffled as she bent her head.

'I have never felt he had gone, not really. It is the same feeling of waiting, I suppose—as though he might come back, not knowing. I have wanted to say goodbye and to feel he was free. It's strange, but, although I would panic at the thought of being without him, I found that when I heard the news of his death there was almost a sense of relief, as though a burden had been lifted.'

'You were strong enough to survive without him this time,' I told her. 'He has been the one who needed to depend so absolutely on you, and it was he who needed the reassurance that

134

he was free to go, and that it was all right. He has waited on that road, outside that building, symbolically, until you came to say goodbye and to send him safely on his way.'

Together we prayed and Vanda spoke quietly to her father, and at the end told me:

'I am so glad, I feel he has gone peacefully now and is at rest.'

The karmic bonds which had kept those two souls tied to each other so that neither was able to achieve its full spiritual potential, had hopefully been broken for good, leaving only voluntary links born of freedom and love.

CHAPTER SEVEN

SESSION CASEBOOK

After each past life session, I have been in the habit of making a report, that sums up briefly the 'lives' we have dealt with and the conclusions we have drawn for the benefit of the sitter. Often, the lives may be sketchy or not particularly memorable. There were many simple people who spent their lifetimes in basic survival, and I have also dealt, for instance, with a larger-than-average number of people who lived in primitive, but seemingly contented conditions in the equivalent of the typical South Sea Island—though, just as often, the volcanic nature of those islands brought sudden tragedy and death.

Many of the cases I have encountered are arbitrary and cannot easily be fitted in to a 'theme' or particular topic, so I have written this chapter as a mini-casebook of a more general nature, illustrating the wide variety of glimpses that may come through past lives. When settling down to a session it is impossible to predict what will emerge, and the results are invariably not what one might have expected.

* * *

Sara regressed in trance to a life where, she told me, she was walking along a path, wearing some type of straw sandals on her feet, and carrying a bundle of straw on her back.

'How old are you?'

'Quite young. About six.'

'Where are you going?'

'Home to my family. Except they're not my family.' (We discussed the possibilities inherent in this cryptic statement afterwards, without being able to deduce what it meant).

'Are you glad to be going home?'

'Very.'

I took her forward ten years, and asked her what she was doing then.

'Gathering food in a market.'

She was very vague, and I asked her whether she still wore sandals on her feet.

'No, sheepskin—little sheepskin boots.'

After a few seconds she said coolly, 'I would like to come back now.'

I brought her safely to the present.

*　　*　　*

Jim, a fellow-psychic, specialized in the use of the runes: those ancient talisman stones that contain the most amazing power. I was appearing at a Psychic Fair where he had been placed near me, and during a lull we spoke together.

'I don't know whether it is the influence of the runes or what,' I told him, 'but I am seeing you in the ancient pagan past—Celtic I think— and your hands and the knives you carry are drenched with blood. The carcasses are all round your feet.'

He smiled.

'Well, I have been wrestling all day with Herne and the Wild Hunt.'

This reference to the 'Horned God' of pagan belief and the great pack of the 'Wild Hunt' that stream across the sky screaming for blood, thrilled me.

'Maybe that, too. But I am seeing you in ancient times. You were not a hunter yourself, you were one of the men who cut up the carcasses. It was hard work—difficult, skilled. And because of the . . . well, whether symbolic or actual blood on your hands, you lived alone.'

He sighed.

'Yes, that sounds like me. Did I ever find a girl to warm my heart?'

I considered, then shook my head slowly.

'Sorry, no. It was intended that you should be alone.'

*   *   *

My notes for Roseanne's past-life session in August 1994 included some extremely unexpected material, part of which I touched on in *A Psychic's Casebook*. I give it here in full.

Life 1: 'Lucy', about 18. An inmate of an asylum in about the 1700s. She is completely withdrawn into her mind; cannot remember relatives, or grass or birds, or any emotion; stones (walls) all around. She was not insane or ill at all when she came; does not know who put her there or why. Frail, weak; probably died of TB.

Life 2: Girl about time of the English Civil war. Happy childhood in a house with tall chimneys and garden. Beautifully dressed; aged about 8; very spoiled.

Then scene changes. (Aged about 14?) Bombardment of a city or town at night. Cannon, guns, horses dying, screaming, houses falling all around. She is lost and running, struggling, trying to find ... (what? who?) [Note: During this link up, Roseanne visualized

138

a dark-haired man present. She said he was silent but wanted to speak. The father who used to spoil her, trying to contact her after having lost her during the bombardment?]

Life 3: Man (young) *c*.100 AD, possibly Roman galley-slave. Wrecked on rocky coast, had to survive. They fought each other; he killed his companions and ate them; ate stones and grass. Went insane; died insane.

* * *

I suggested that Roseanne's past lives indicated a reluctance to accept the dark side of existence as part of the whole picture, a tendency to try to escape into the mind—also a preoccupation with the solitary and with the loneliness of the spirit. She needed, I felt, to accept that a situation could be viewed from a positive as well as a negative angle, that one could learn even from painful experiences, and that blocking off or running away provided no real answer.

* * *

Justin, a powerful healer who often felt more at home in the realms of the spirit than coping with earthly difficulties, was someone whose work I had respected and admired for a long time. When we sat down for a past-life session, I would not have been surprised to discover that he had previously existed as a saint, or even the Archangel Gabriel. But the three lives that emerged were very different.

'I get a dark, rocky coast . . . very foggy, with this heavy mist rolling in from the sea. The Portuguese coast, maybe, or Spanish—but a long time ago. You seem to have lived there alone, in an extremely desolate place, and there was . . . not a lighthouse, nor even a house at all, but some kind of marker or fire that you kept burning. I think you lived very rough, like a type of hermit. Nobody else about at all, nothing but this dark, foggy night and the fire.'

His second life came as quite a shock.

'I have you during the time of the Pharaohs in ancient Egypt, though I can't be more specific than that. You were a man, but some sort of beautician; you were responsible for the make-up and hair of the women in the royal house. You spent most of your time with the women. I see you moving about with mirrors and curling tongs and you were quite different to the hermit: very gossipy and chatty and full of merry quips, like a kind of court jester. You wore a short tunic, and you moved quickly. You were lithe and used your hands a lot, and seemed the life and soul of the party.'

Justin was intrigued, commenting that the picture did not seem to be one he could easily identify with.

'I think you could, though, because, under the quips and the naughty court gossip, this

140

man was utterly alone. He was just as alone as the hermit on the cliffs, and just as desolate within his heart. And I feel he was very aware— even though he might have held a highly regarded position—that he was, under it all, just a slave, an object.'

'He put on a mask? That is interesting. I know what you mean.' Justin considered the prospect. 'Yes, in some ways that is even more near to the truth than an obvious alienation as a hermit. I have often felt it is difficult to belong, even when surrounded by people.'

His third life again emphasized his difficulties in relating to the problems of every day on the human level. It found him as an old man, crippled and aged, abandoned on a seashore, alone.

'Everyone else has gone; I think they were trying to escape some disaster. They have all left, run screaming away as it were, before the disaster strikes—evacuated the place. Nobody was bothered about you, and you were too weak and feeble to go with them. It must have been an early civilization—I can't identify it. You are just there, waiting, left to cope alone and to face the disaster that is to come.'

* * *

Raffina, a very attractive lady whose children had grown up and left home, was now alone and felt she wanted to begin a new, more positive phase of her life. She consulted me first for a tarot reading to give her directions for the future. She seemed to possess great potential, and I asked whether she had thought of setting up some sort of business of her own; I suggested something artistic and creative.

'I am getting . . . not exactly embroidery, but tapestries, rich tapestry work,' I told her. 'Have you ever felt drawn to anything like this?'

'I can sew, but I have never thought of tapestries,' she said, wonderingly. 'I do love fabrics, though, the richness and texture and colour. In fact, I am thinking of signing up for a course in Fabric and Design in a few weeks.'

I told her that in a past life, she had been the chatelaine of a great house in medieval France—a lady of power and influence, surrounded by beautiful things, familiar with the making of tapestries—and that this knowledge would stand her in good stead today for her business. I approved of the course she wanted to take, and she left after what seemed to have been a brisk and interesting session.

Some months later, I had forgotten the interview when she contacted me again and came to see me once more.

'There are so many things I want to tell you which related to what you told me,' she said. 'But particularly about . . . remember the past life when you said I had lived in France in a château—the lady with the tapestries? Well, I had no knowledge of France previously, but

142

this summer, I went there, and one day there was an outing to a château—I don't remember its name, and I didn't take much notice at the time.

'But I went, and I found that I was recognizing the places, and I recognized the buildings. It was weird, I can't account for it. It seemed like I was going back to somewhere I knew well.'

* * *

A gift from the past seemed apparent when I was doing a reading for Valery. I held her hands.

'You were regarded as a witch at some time in the past,' I told her, and we joked together. As I have already said, so-called 'witches' were apparently numerous, sometimes regarded with fear, often badly treated.

'You actually did have powers to heal illness, and in fact you still have the gifts in your hands,' I went on. 'Strangely, you were not a healer as such, but you had the ability to gather and mix the medicines—a "feel" for herbs, plants, leaves, and so on, that would cure. The ability is here very strongly, and you could do this now if you wanted to apply yourself to herbs and healing. There is no healing power actually in your fingers, no ability to heal by laying on of hands, but the way you have with herbs and plants, the way you would intuitively

143

gather, select and mix the ingredients would make the results seem like magic.'

Valery was interested, but unimpressed. I thought that if she could feel the power of her own ability in her fingers as I could, she would have had a very different opinion of herself. People had not regarded her in her past lives as able to perform 'miraculous' cures without good reason.

* * *

Another 'witch' emerged during a session with Alys. As soon as I linked in to the past, I was able to see that she had been done to death at least twice: once stoned, and the second time beaten with cudgels.

'You were not really a witch at all, though, in any sense,' I said. 'You were retarded, deformed, of limited intelligence: a sullen, ungainly, lumpish girl—under five feet—and you were persecuted because you were not like the rest. You also seem to have had a vengeful nature, so that the feeling I get lingering from the deaths is not fear or pain but something very negative about getting your own back: "making them pay". It's rather pathetic, really, that the only comfort this poor creature had in her life and after it was the thought that she would somehow take her miseries out on everybody else and make them suffer as well.'

The presence of this girl-woman was so

strong that I could see the darkness surrounding her like a stain across Alys's aura, and I became increasingly certain that she had not found rest. She was still occupying a large portion of Alys's present persona, and I told Alys that, if she agreed, we would free the unhappy spirit and help it to leave her for the light where it belonged.

In the meantime I linked in for some other life, to see whether I could find anything except 'Maera' or 'Maire' (the girl-woman's name) in Alys's past. I saw a softly rippling inland lake with a pebble beach, and she was a child, walking alone beside the water; there was nothing else around except thick forest in all directions, and the sun hanging heavily in a red haze on the horizon. I had the impression that this had been in some Scandinavian country— very far north—and that there had been other people, but they were hidden behind the forest barrier. The child had existed in its own mind, alone.

She asked whether the place could have been in the north of Scotland—she had in fact recognized the scene as the shore of a private sea-loch, where she wandered alone when visiting friends.

'I seemed to know it the first time I ever went there,' she said. 'You have described it exactly.'

Alys had on either side of her, in this life, two child images from the past. The pitiful figure of 'Maera' had never been able to cope. The child beside the water was too young.

'I think you have always felt you were a child, within yourself. And while they are with you, you will not be able to grow to the adult serenity and calm which is waiting for you. They have tried their best, but it is time for you to let them go now. You have a wonderful, shining potential, but while they are with you you will never be able to achieve it fully.'

Alys accepted this, and together, we set about taking the 'children' home. Prayers, a lighted candle, and she led the way down the stairs of her flat to where the lobby door had been left open. She lit them on their way, and when we returned to her living-room she gave a sigh.

'I do feel . . . I feel very much lighter. As though something has happened.'

People in this situation are often emotionally overcome, and she leaned on me and let me hold her quietly for a few minutes.

'I will get flowers for her, later.'

'And the child. You can be yourself now, completely you, the woman, when you go back to the shore of the loch.'

* * *

I could find nothing that seemed familiar when I linked in for Liza.

'You don't seem to be human at all. You

seem like some sort of wraith-like figure, wrapped in a long robe, drifting over landscapes, continents, looking down. I can see great rivers—they seem to mean something—like the Ganges, and there are women washing their clothes on the big flat stones. Have you any connection with India or that part of the world?'

Liza could not identify with this.

'I get a feeling of great sadness,' I told her. 'You do not want to come down and join in, but at the same time, you can find no place where you will feel you belong. It seems as though you are not a human being but have come from somewhere else. I might even say you are some sort of prophet or lesser deity, who is looking for his followers or the place where he will be recognized and can carry out the work he is to do. I think you have felt this within yourself.'

'I feel I have potential that hasn't been used,' she said honestly.

'There is a very high potential. Don't be afraid of recognizing this —it is a fact. You are probably a superior soul to myself, for instance. But let's try another life. We might get something clearer.'

The second life was equally mystifying.

'I cannot get a person once again. I have an image in my mind of a ship, a sort of whaler, stuck in snow and ice. It is not damaged, it is just stuck against the ice. Somewhere like the South Pole, Antarctica. The ice is very bright, and the scene is very clear. But there is nobody on the ship, it is quite deserted. I don't know where they are—simply that it is empty and still. Does that mean anything to you?'

Liza was finding the whole thing just as puzzling as I.

'There is something else, though,' I told her. 'There is some life there, but it is not people. There are dogs—big dogs, like huskies, with thick coats, tearing at a carcase of seal meat or some sort of animal meat. There is blood all around on the ice, bright red. I don't know where it came from, the meat, but they are eating it.'

I was unable to find her a persona; she had not been a dog, nor, I thought, the dead seal. But the same sense of wandering, of having no place, seemed to be present. I thought she had a destiny, involving higher spiritual activity and awareness, which she had not yet begun to explore. I felt that the body seemed to pull her down against her will (she revealed, towards the end of the session, that she was just recovered from several serious operations). But mainly I felt she was a representative of the divine, and that in this capacity she suffered the loneliness and spiritual isolation that such beings must undergo. She said she had started to study psychic and spiritual activity, and I warned her that she had as yet only begun to scratch the surface of what was to be (apart from her already successful career in fashion) her life's work.

* * *

Jackie's past life appeared dimly: shadows being thrown onto a kind of canvas wall by leaping flames. It was a tent, I thought, in a rough barracks, an army on the move.

'There were soldiers, maybe four, even more,' I said. 'And though I can only see the shadows, that's perhaps as well. You were a sort of camp-follower, and you were there in the middle of them, on the floor, a bundle of flesh and skirts, being passed from one to another, just anybody's. There was a lot of noise and yelling, rough handling, probably drink and violence. You were used to it. This was the life you knew … how you survived. You were tough, hard as nails—you had to be. And yet somewhere the hurt of being just a thing, a possession to be used, went in very deep. You felt like an abused child too, as though you had never been given a chance.'

She nodded, thinking it over.

'I can relate to that. My life has been … well, tough, as you say.'

A few days later, when I saw her again, she told me excitedly that she had been considering her life as a camp follower, and had begun to relate to it even more than on first hearing.

'I think it was absolutely right,' she added. 'I

feel I have been living that sort of life again, being used and having no sense of my own worth. And those soldiers who abused me, they are in this life. I have identified them—all four of them—in this present existence.'

* * *

'I don't usually accept visions of Red Indian Chiefs, in full war-bonnet and war-paint,' I told Martin, smiling. 'It is far too clichéd an image. But in your case it is so clear and vivid that I cannot mistake it. You were someone of historical standing, though I can't give you a name, and you led your people to the death, renowned and respected by the white men as well as your own kind. I see you at a moment in a great battle—Little Big Horn? No, that was where the Indians won, wasn't it?—but some great battle. You had turned your head under the great war bonnet and were looking round at the way the battle was going, seeming to actually hold your people physically to your heart, your compassion for them all tearing at you in such a way it actually hurt.'

Martin, though mildly flattered, did not regard himself in this kind of light. He said he had never thought of being a great leader, and had no particular empathy for the culture of the North American Indians.

'This man was immensely wise, probably through lifetimes of acquiring wisdom,' I told

150

him. 'You have the powers within you at the moment—I could tell from your hands. But you are not confident enough to use them, or do not feel the time has yet come. You are either having a rest this time round (a "day off" as it were) or else you are going to find that you mature later in your life and will be given this sort of responsibility.'

He was a practising homeopathic doctor, a qualified reflexologist and an aromatherapist, among other things. I felt, and told him, that he was already applying his theory and knowledge, but that the wisdom he had possessed in his past lives and the strong spiritual power would balance his ability to give and would transform it into a deep, true greatness. And yet, I sensed that there was a good deal of hesitancy. We tried a second life.

'I am getting two images,' I said. 'And in the same way as the Red Indian chief, you have brought me to another cliché era: ancient Egypt, or possibly Mesopotamia or Babylon, or somewhere similar, in ancient times—it is difficult to tell. And these images could be divided by centuries, as well as thousands of miles, though they seem so alike.'

The first was a man sitting at a desk in a painted room, writing onto a piece of papyrus.

'I thought it was a library, but it is not—just a quiet room, with painted panels and a low ceiling. He is making a record of something very learned: theories, or experiments, or the

151

results of his thinking. I suppose he has similar characteristics to the chief—wise, learned and, in his case, detached. The other image is quite different.

'I saw an animal first of all: a lion, chained so that it could move and walk up and down a decorated marble pavement. Not free to escape, though. Just up and down, up and down. I thought at first you were the lion—it is a very beautiful creature with tawny fur and a thick mane—and then I saw there was someone else present. The lion had a keeper, a companion: an adolescent youth in a thin tunic that reached below his knees, white with purple edges. You were the keeper. And, since you lived and slept with the lion, you almost regarded it as an extension of yourself, or the other way about . . . projected yourself into it.'

Martin was listening, his eyes closed.

'I thought it was the lion I was picking up, how it felt about being able to pace only up and down, up and down. But I can see now that it was the boy, the keeper, who identified himself with the power and strength of that beautiful creature and felt for it, that it should be chained and a prisoner. I have no idea what the lion really felt. The boy submerged himself into it, so that it is difficult for me to see which was which—or if they had become the same.'

Though Martin did not feel there was anything he could immediately relate to his own position, I felt as we neared the close of

152

the sitting that he had a similar dichotomy within himself. He possessed the great powers I had seen in the chief, but when I had held his hands as we began the session, I had felt, beneath the potential, a great humility.

'As though you came to offer yourself for service, but felt you had nothing to give,' I told him. 'You do not believe in your spiritual powers, do you?'

'No, I suppose I do doubt,' he admitted.

'There is no need,' I said. 'They are there, whenever you choose to use them. But your humility, the genuine lack of personal pride, is one of the great gifts—the mark of spiritual elevation. You do not need to identify with others, or compare yourself. The man to whom those hesitating, humble hands belong has no need of apology.'

* * *

Kara, a slim and graceful girl with long, dark hair, emerged from our first linking-up with the past as almost a legend.

'A matador?' she echoed in surprise.

'Yes, but more than just a matador. Someone who risked his life fighting the bulls in this ritual in order to challenge fate, or even God. As though he wanted to prove something and could not. There is a sense of equality, as though he and God—his God, his fate, or whatever one calls it—were trying to master each other. And he wanted fate (or God) to win—to take him in the bull-ring, so that he could feel he had met his match, been bested by a stronger force. But fate refused to give him this satisfaction; he did not die in the ring, and he was more and more frustrated and baffled.'

Kara recognized within herself the driving force and fearless, masculine qualities possessed by the matador—and the sensation of confronting and trying to control her destiny, yet at the same time being aware that there was much she did not understand. We went on to a second life.

'A girl,' I said. 'A little girl, alone—I think from a boat that has crashed into the bank of a wide lake—wandering through a forest on her own.'

I felt this life had something to do with Russia, though Kara had no Russian connections. It seemed to tell us little, except that the child had been left to cope alone. We passed on to another existence, and here I told Kara that there was no need to say anything.

'The Russian connection seemed to be a lost princess or royal child, though it was vague. This time there is no doubt of the royal blood. You were a queen, somewhere like Babylon, ancient Egypt, somewhere in the east. The sensation of royalty—of having inherited it in the blood, rather than marrying into it or grabbing it by force—is very strong. Even then you were royal, and by the time you reached the matador, you had had plenty of time to develop mental as well as physical eminence.'

CHAPTER EIGHT

PAST LIFE THERAPY AND THE CASE OF TANYA B

What is the use of going back to the past, I am sometimes asked. Isn't it the present that matters? What difference can the past make? We cannot change what has happened—or can we?

I have already touched on the ways in which awareness of previous existence can help those who carry with them some problem, some difficulty in relating to life, to others or to themselves. In general, this sort of therapy happens almost naturally, and the benefits are clearly seen. Even if they are not put into practice by the sufferer, the messages are there and can act as a sort of instruction-book in the future, whenever the person concerned feels ready to move on and apply them.

There are, however, far more serious cases, where it does almost seem that the journey back into the past is going to involve some drastic change—something indeed being altered, or, in whatever way possible, put right.

155

When considering such cases, the question that arises is whether—even if we find the right place and time—anything in the past can be changed. It has already happened; how, then, can we change it? In science fiction this problem of 'trying to stop Abe Lincoln getting shot' or 'saving my comrade in the Crimea (except that, if I did, I would alter the whole course of my life and would probably not have been born in the present at all, or be here now)' can assume huge and interesting proportions. It is a fascinating thought: could we, if we could return to the past, become Cleopatra's lover and oust Mark Antony, or stop the St Valentine's Day Massacre, or save Marilyn?

The answer is, of course, No. Nothing that has already happened in linear time can be changed, not by a fraction. But what can be changed is our perception of what happened, and our attitude to it. Sometimes this can seem just as miraculous as if the past itself had been completely altered. When this kind of therapy is applied the person concerned can seem to change as though he has shed a skin, like a snake, or emerged from a chrysalis into a completely new being. It is a visible part of the process of spiritual growth, and can be difficult and painful. But the new being that results from such wrestling with the past will be stronger and wiser, purified and refined by the ordeal.

When dealing with past trauma in current lifetimes, practitioners sometimes use a process called *abreaction*. This involves regressing the patient, either under hypnosis or with the use of drugs, to the traumatic event and allowing him to relive it and deal with it *as it happened at that time*. The effect is as though the patient is able to live the incident over again and, this time, resolve the trauma. Deeply buried memories that have been blanked out by the personality as too painful to face can thus be coped with and removed from their festering place in the unconscious—and with them go the patterns of defensive behaviour with which the personality has tried to protect itself. The result can be so drastic that the 'new' person that emerges needs to shed his whole lifestyle—and sometimes his relationships—in order to find the place where he rightfully belongs.

Similar traumas may be carried from past existence, and can be dealt with in a similar manner, though they can sometimes seem too glib. One fellow-practitioner recounted to me the case of a woman patient who had a phobia about being shut in rooms and always insisted on having the door open; in regression she described how in a past life she had been buried alive as a young child. Each case must be judged on its merits and on the outcome, whether positive and helpful or merely frivolous. If a phobia is dealt with satisfactorily, and the patient's well-being increases (for whatever reason) then the therapy can only be regarded as successful—however it has been worked.

* * *

Tanya B's case is an extreme example of how past-life therapy can work in an almost miraculous manner, and it reveals interesting details of the process itself. Tanya, a successful writer, was able to detach herself from her mental problems while passing through a form of 'therapy', and not only recorded how she thought and felt while it was proceeding but was able to give an objective assessment of what happened and to draw conclusions.

Suffering from undiagnosed manic-depressive psychosis, and having twice attempted suicide, she began in her mid-forties to write what was to turn into a dark journey, not only into her current life but into her previous existence.

'I had no idea of what I was doing, or where I was going,' she says. 'I thought I might never return—that I might just go completely insane and lose all touch with reality—but I felt that, although I had no medical supervision, I had to carry on. There was nowhere else to go, so I had to keep going forward.'

Two people knew what Tanya was doing: the partner she lived with, Jacko, and her long-standing writing friend Charlotte. Both knew she had serious mental problems, and, though neither was medically qualified, they gave her loyal and generous support.

'My book—the record I was writing (and reliving as I did it)—seemed to go back to my childhood first,' she recalls. 'All the hidden things I couldn't face came out, and the anger and pain that I had suppressed. I could hardly stand the feelings that came back, and I kept thinking that I had to have reached the end . . . I mean, I had gone back to my earliest memories—where else was there? I never thought for a minute of trying to go back to a past life; it just didn't seem to occur to me. I don't think I would have accepted the idea anyway. So what did happen came without my conscious awareness, and I didn't connect it with the past—not then. I got a different image for it in my mind. I thought of it as a "descent into the depths", into some dreadful dark place inside myself. But, when you look at it, it is quite obviously another existence—though even now I don't know quite what.'

'Your account reveals that, unconsciously, you were putting yourself into states of self-hypnosis. You call it "going back" but in fact you were reliving the past as it happened, experiencing all the painful emotions you had felt at the time.'

'Oh, yes,' she agrees fervently. 'Sometimes I felt so ill from anger or . . . or fear, I suppose, that I had never learned how to cope with. I was physically sick at the thought of myself as a small child. I had been frightened all my life, but just struggled through as best I could. I would shake—literally shake so much I couldn't write—just thinking back.'

'Did it help?' I query.

'I don't know,' she says honestly. 'I would not have dared to try and go back at all if I had realized just how painful it would be—although while I was in it, it was like trying to rise to the surface of deep water: once I started off, I couldn't stop until I came out at the top, as it were. The whole thing was like an avalanche: once I took one step, the process could not be halted. I think this is important for people to know, so they understand that this kind of therapy is not a game or something you can mess about with. Once you have taken that first step you are committed, and there is no way you can turn back. If there is pain, you have to go through it, and there are no short cuts or ways round.'

Throughout the experience—which lasted for some six weeks at its most intense—Charlotte acted as a 'sounding board' for Tanya's thoughts, feelings and theories, and they used to chat on the phone each evening about the progress Tanya had made that day. Their discussions were occasionally recorded, and sometimes Tanya would write up what she had to say in the form of an edited conversation

160

from the tapes. The account which follows is as she wrote it for her record, her 'book'.

The Case of Tanya B.

(Extract from Tanya's conversation with Charlotte.)

Charlotte: Tanya, I know that writing this book . . . what you are doing . . . has been—still is—intensely traumatic.

Tanya: Yes, in fact I'm not at all sure whether I'm helping myself to uncover the traumas of the past and hopefully face them, or whether I'm driving myself further into stark raving insanity, where I shall be lost for evermore. I have been having feelings I've never experienced before, which may or may not be some new sort of depression—there are different types of depressions, as you know, having suffered yourself.

Charlotte: A sort of black pit?

Tanya: The colour goes out of the world.

Charlotte: You slow down; nothing's ever going to be right.

Tanya: An absolute despair. I know it so well, almost a way of life—and, although you know it will pass, it seems as though it never will. You get to understanding the way it works . . . but, apart from that, I've also been experiencing—possibly through consciously trying to think myself into my problems—other sensations that I thought at first were different, new

161

depressions . . . but I'm not sure now whether they're actually depressions at all. I can't really say what they are.

Charlotte: Can you describe them?

Tanya: Not very clearly. They've been coming so slowly that I didn't notice them to start with, but the other day I had the worst one so far, and I tried to describe it afterwards . . . tried to write down what it had felt like. This is what I wrote:

I thought I'd touched bottom, the depths—but now the bottom gets deeper, the depths of lostness and pain become unfathomable. I can't speak, I can't scream or cry or hold onto anything or anyone. My whole body is a mute vessel into which the pain pours, fills to the brim, cannot express itself. I have no words, no tears, I ache—throb—exist as a single unit of pain. This is past despair, past desperation, depression, past the sickness of the soul that I thought I could not bear. I have known nothing like it. It is not living, it is not death. There are no words for me to describe it; I cannot compare it to anything. It is so utterly, utterly negative, such a state of sick nothingness that no images I can conjure up are powerful enough. Agony is positive; it provokes a reaction. This provokes nothing. It is the unendurable, which I must endure until I can find the strength to struggle free, to come back to words, consciousness of reality.

That's so inadequate, though, Charlotte. I was floundering, I simply couldn't use words which would describe the feeling—I couldn't find any. It seemed a sort of sensation . . . experience . . . whatever it was . . . that was absolutely, completely unfamiliar. As though I'd been somewhere . . . some place . . . that I had never, ever known in my life. It certainly wasn't death. I was not dying; I wasn't dead, but it was some . . . I can't even find the right words now. I could . . . not . . . utter—no sound. The comparisons, the images I tried to think of were simply . . . oh, removed, just utterly removed. I thought of . . . oh, the Arctic—wolves howling—and then said, 'No, that's much, much too positive—trapped animals'. None of that actually explained it, got anywhere near it. I thought of a shriek of pain, a scream of pain—but there *was* no shriek, no scream. I can't even find one right word for 'it', whatever or wherever it was or might have been. Just pain, nothingness, lostness, awfulness . . . None of them is right.

Charlotte: There were no physical familiarities?

Tanya: No. It was very frightening, because it seemed a place that I'd never ever conceived or known of, or imagined. I couldn't begin to describe it at all. And it was worse for being unable to be expressed in any way of which my five senses are capable. It can't be expressed in any other form than by living it. That's all I can say, really. But what I was living, I don't know.

* * *

In the same conversation Tanya and Charlotte discussed the actual procedure by which Tanya had made her link with this other 'experience' or 'existence'. The account reveals that she attempted to give as honest a record as she could, but was completely unaware of the possible significance of what she said.

Charlotte: How did you feel when you came out of it? Have you any idea how long it lasted? Tanya: I don't think it was very long, because I made an effort—I tried to . . . well, come back, I suppose. In the beginning, everything faded, and I was able to take in very little of what was going on around me. In depression, of course, one normally isn't very interested, but this wasn't so much not being interested, it was as though everything faded into the distance. I might have been spoken to; if I was, I don't think I answered. I couldn't speak. And afterwards I had a reaction that took the form of . . . well, not speaking. I wanted to speak, but I was afraid I couldn't get back to the words, use my voice. I couldn't speak for . . . oh, half an hour. I was crying, even though I wasn't really crying . . . a few very slight tears running down my face. I wanted to cry and I couldn't, because I couldn't express myself in any way. I could move; I could walk, but only if I was led. I knew I'd got to come back and . . . well, I felt as though I couldn't really hold onto anything, even though Jacko sat with me.

I shook, quite violently . . . gasped, took big gulps, as though I'd been drowning and come up for air. Eventually, it all wore off. But that was my reaction, it wasn't the 'thing'. I had got perhaps half-way back by then. What I wanted more than anything was to be able to cry. I knew, or felt, that by being able to cry I would be making contact with normality, and I'd have to cry something out. And I did say to Jacko . . . it's not easy to remember what happened now . . . I said, 'I've been very far away. I've been very deep.' I said, 'It is much more painful than I thought, there is a lot of pain somewhere down there.' And then I said, 'Terrible, terrible pain,' and after I managed to say just those few words, get them out, I was able to cry.'

'And what was your conclusion at the time?' I ask Tanya. 'What did you think had happened? Where did you think you had "been"?'

'We discussed it, Charlotte and I, and the general opinion seemed to be that I had returned to a time before I was born, maybe in the womb. It seemed to be the only solution that would explain away the state I went to: unable to express myself through my senses,

165

alive but not alive in the way I knew it. I also felt, though I forgot to include it in the book, that there was no gravity and that I was "floating". Do you think it could have been that?'

I thought that was certainly a possibility, but asked, 'Now you know more, and a few years have passed since this happened, could you accept that you might have returned to a past existence in order to "lay your ghosts"? The fact that you did it on your own does not matter—and what actually caused the pain is not really relevant. But I do find the part you describe as "coming back" of more significance than you and Charlotte realized at the time. When a person is regressed, even to heavy trauma like this, they do not generally take hours to return to the present, especially if, as in your case, you were aware with one part of your mind that you had to return and were making a conscious and determined effort to do so.'

Tanya was puzzled.

'What do you think it was, then?'

I told her that, purely on the evidence of the book, read some years later, it was difficult to be sure, but that the part she described as 'coming back' seemed to me to be part of the regression itself.

'I think you regressed yourself to this terrible trauma—whatever and whenever it happened.' I told her. 'And then, still regressed, you went into the severe shock which would have followed. The symptoms you describe would be applicable if this was the case. Then you actually had to bring yourself back not only from a past existence, but from a traumatic state of shock. The fact that you did so successfully was a quite remarkable feat to have accomplished on your own.'

She flushed.

'I know it was not a sensible thing to do—but I had been trying for years to sort out my mind with self-help. I was able to be very detached, very strong. And I honestly don't think I would have gone to . . . wherever it was . . . just like that, sitting at the kitchen table after supper, unless my mind was ready to cope with it. I did not do it consciously, it just happened.'

Normally, I would never advise anyone to try such difficult regressions in problematical states of mind, unless under very competent supervision—but there are always exceptions, and Tanya was one of them. For her past-life trauma, revisited alone, did help, though as a part of a much wider relearning process and perception of reality revealed in the whole, book-length manuscript that recorded her six weeks of intense, private mental activity.

If anyone ever doubted the ability of past-life therapy miraculously to change painful circumstances, Tanya's words affirm that it can and has been done. At the end of her 'book' she made this affirmation:

I realize now that all through my life it has been a case of 'this is the way things are— you must accept them'. And I wouldn't accept them. I fought and fought, though vaguely aware in sick desperation that, even if I succeeded in rejecting them, I would be no better off. It was a classic of what is called a double-bind—a no-win situation.

'You *must* accept them,' said somebody— God, I suppose. And I cried back, equally relentlessly, 'I will *not* accept them.' 'You must live', said God. 'I won't', I screamed. 'I'll die'. And I ended up unable to do either. And all the time, the answer was there, but I was not able to see it. It isn't a question of 'You *must* accept this'. I may not want to accept it; I may still want to fight it; I may not like it. But how different, how amazingly, wonderfully different if I had realized that I actually have a choice. The alternative to 'This is the way things are—I must accept them' is: 'This is the way things are—I can *choose* to accept them'. Even the bad things, the difficult things, the things I don't want.

In going back to that original primitive pain, the deep hurt that was still tormenting me in the depths of my mind, I didn't have it forced on me this time. It wasn't a case of the little entity thinking, 'This is hurting and I don't like it. If this is the way things are, I reject them. I don't want to know.' It wasn't a case of God, or whoever, saying, 'Well, you've got no choice, mate; you're stuck with it, whether you like it or not.' But when the original pain, hurt, rejection happened, that was what I felt, and that was what I experienced again when I went back. I didn't want things the way they were; I turned the other way; I fought them. And all my life, I have been doing the same thing.

But if only that previous entity had been able to say to itself: 'Yes, well, I don't like this hurt, but I suppose it's the way things are. I can't change it so I suppose I'll have to accept it for now. It might go away soon.'

When I went back, I deliberately—insofar as I was able—opened my mind to the pain. I *chose* to go back and accept it. If I *choose* to accept other seemingly unbearable and unacceptable facts, they appear so much more in proportion. I do not need to torment myself with them any more. I cannot alter them. I *choose* to accept their inevitability. And so I can *choose* to accept all the things I have been fighting against for so long. It will not change them; they cannot be changed—this is the way things are. But I can *choose* to accept that they cannot be altered, and I can concentrate instead on what *can* be altered to put things right, make things easier and better. I couldn't alter the world, but by writing this record and going through all it involved—making my own decision to do it—I have altered myself. And found that I can choose now to accept the world as it is, myself as I am.'

The manuscript is signed and dated 'Tanya B. London. October 1987'. Tanya now works as a counsellor and therapist.

CHAPTER NINE

PAST LIFE AS ANIMALS

As we have seen from the case histories in this book, it is quite possible for a past life to have been spent in four-footed, or even furred or finned form—though one never knows when this may happen, and it is impossible to predict. But my experience indicates overwhelmingly that the souls of human beings—those divine flames that never die and remain eternally contained within themselves—may well have passed through previous incarnations where they occupied the outward shapes of cats, bears, insects, or creatures unfamiliar to us now. Cases I have previously mentioned in *A Psychic's Casebook* include a timid beast from prehistoric times, as well as my own regression to a thin, stray, ginger cat in Victorian London. There are many questions that I am regularly asked about animals, their souls or lack of souls, and where they stand in relation to human beings, so far as spiritual development goes. Religious theories propound several concepts that apply here. One is that all souls start off at the bottom of the ladder, as it were, as something very insignificant, like an ant or even a microbe. According to this theory, each life is a learning process that, if wisely applied, will allow the soul to rise each time into a higher life-form—maybe a rat or a fish or a snake—until enough wisdom has been acquired for the soul to enter the realms of humanity and be born as a man or woman. Then it must apply itself to attaining spiritual enlightenment, so that it can climb even higher and eventually achieve the ultimate, which is nirvana: a state of complete perfection and bliss, union with the Buddha.

A second theory (in much simplified form, of course) propounds more of a see-saw principle. If we live a beastly, gluttonous existence now, we will condemn ourselves to return in our next life as, say, a wild boar. We will then have to re-earn our place as a human being. This idea incorporates the laws of karma, according to which the soul must pay for its bad deeds and is rewarded for the good. The aim in the end is the same: to achieve complete union with the absolute. A third theory tells us that each life is judged on its own merits, and that what happened previously has no bearing on what is to come.

So where do animals come in, so far as evidence from case histories is concerned? One thing is certain: it is impossible to regress an animal to ask whether it has been a human being in a previous life. However, there is quite a lot of evidence to show that human sitters have previously existed as animals—though (in my experience) in a random way, rather than as a direct process of learning and rising up the biological tree. Little work has been done on this subject, probably because, as I have said, it is impossible to know when a past life will take the form of something other than a human being. Also, communication with previous existence as an animal might prove difficult for some practitioners. It is necessary to keep an open mind at all levels.

The time-span—(or possible absence of time) in relation to human/animal incarnations is very important when considering whether development follows any order of progression. Gerry's past existence as a spider, for instance, could have happened at any time, and her life as a tormented gorilla might have been a 'step up' towards a human incarnation. This could mean that she *had* progressed up the biological tree. In my own case, my life as a thin cat—which could be dated by the boots worn by the men in the Victorian public house, and by the streets I saw—was quite recent, and I have experienced other, chronologically 'earlier' lives in which I was a human being. However, if we imagine the past, present and future happening simultaneously, then none of this careful working out of sequences has any meaning at all.

In general, though, my experience seems to indicate that, however the spiritual progress of the soul is measured, it is quite possible for animal life to alternate with human lives, and in no particular order. This would appear to confirm that animals—to whatever extent—do possess souls, since the soul in such cases would pass through every incarnation, including animal lives.

*   *   *

Linking up for Tina, I tell her I can see a large kitchen, as though belonging to a big country house, in the Elizabethan period.

'A high window or windows, so that the kitchen itself might have been in a basement, though there is greenery and blue sky visible. There is a big fire, with a spit and something cooking . . . the fat dripping, a lot of preparations of food round the walls, and the implements that would have been used. But the room itself seems empty. There is nobody there, and you are viewing the scene from . . . it looks like the top of a scrubbed table, or that level. You are a cat, a big comfortable cat, and I am seeing everything through your eyes. You know everything is all right, you are familiar with what goes on in the kitchen, and you are viewing your own particular kingdom, quite content with life. I am rather surprised that a cat would have been allowed to settle on a table, but you might have been sitting on a top of a chair or something else.'

I am also surprised that a large kitchen in a busy household should have been empty, with no sign of life, but Tina, who has been familiar with country house life in her childhood, is not.

'There is usually a time—a few minutes maybe—in the afternoon when a kitchen might be empty. Between lunch-time and the evening. I expect it was the same in Elizabethan days too.'

Her second life is a brief, happy glimpse.

'I am getting yellow—vivid yellow flowers on the bushes—and you were a little, dark-haired child, splashing in a river . . . loving it, enjoying the light on the water and just being at that moment. Somewhere in the southern hemisphere, though I can't say how long ago. A thousand years? Two thousand? Time doesn't alter much in that sort of place.'

An interesting picture is emerging of innocence and an untouched quality that I feel Tina carries within her. I proceed to a third life.

'Nets,' I say after a few moments of concentration. 'Fishing nets. I get a child—a boy—mending the nets, or helping to mend them. He is the son of a fisherman, in a fishing

174

village . . . Portuguese, I think.'

Try as I may, there seems to be little more to see, and I feel frustrated because the message from all three lives together is hardly more than an impression. Then I begin to see a vision of a fourth life—or, rather, to hear it.

'Animals shrieking. They are caught in gin traps in the night, and you are a child, turning your face to the wall in your small rough-walled room, trying not to listen. You can do nothing, but your heart is bleeding for them, and you are carrying their suffering and pain yourself.'

At the same time, I feel as though the child is caught within the nets, and the injured and dying animals represent her own torment and struggle as she tries to break free. I have the message now. Tina's qualities of youthful innocence, compassion and vulnerability have made her the sweet-natured person she is in this life, but she needs to detach herself from the suffering of others and be more ruthless about satisfying her own needs. There is still a lot for her to learn in order to wean herself away from the emotional immaturity that has her trapped in the difficulties and demands of others.

* * *

I have found, interestingly, that when linking up with an incarnation that has taken an animal form (and these have so far included cats,

175

bears, a donkey, Gerry's gorilla, and one or two odd creatures difficult to identify) the scope of the soul, though present, has been different to that of a human soul. It is as though the animal is restricted to one, or at the most two, levels of awareness, rather than the many-faceted awareness that marks human sensitivity—as though it lives one-dimensionally.

Picking up Tina's Elizabethan cat, I sensed its satisfaction as it surveyed its 'kingdom', the good feeling that came from knowing it was 'lord of the kitchen'. When I regressed to being a cat myself I was aware that, though I had no particular home, nothing much to eat, there was nothing to worry about. There seemed to be a strong impression that all was well. Gerry's gorilla, in a painful situation, suffered her imprisonment uncomplainingly and waited.

In fact, the sensation that comes over most strongly from an animal 'life' is of unquestioning acceptance. Animals do not worry about tomorrow, next week, or life assurance. They are unable to appreciate that there is a future at all. Neither do they ask 'Why me?', or feel they deserve better treatment, or want to join a trade union. Their 'ego' is geared for survival but, beyond that, is unselfish. They know only the moment, accepting it if it is good, and, if it is not, coping with it as best they can or enduring it.

It is in this simplistic attitude, perhaps, that the message for those who regress to animal lives exists. Animals are unable to work things out rationally, and they have extremely restricted powers of thought. They accept and they trust. If they are betrayed, they accept the betrayal without blame or malice or holding grudges.

In fact, it is interesting to note that indications are emerging from the cases involving animal regressions that I have so far dealt with that such past lives—emphasizing trust, acceptance and unquestioning faith— seem to occur for people who have some sort of emotional difficulty which impairs their ability to trust easily. The past life as animal takes them back to the source, as it were, or provides a point of reference, a simplistic demonstration of how trust can be achieved and how it works.

*　*　*

Often the regression to an animal conveys a confused and, for want of a better word, 'dumb' feeling. When doing a sitting for Rona, I found myself in her past as a hunted deer, just about to be brought down by the hounds in a scene that looked medieval.

'It is difficult,' I told her. 'Difficult to know which is the hunter (other animals seem to be involved—a wolf, for instance), and I see the deer now from a position above, where the spirit would hover if it had just left the body. It is almost as though this whole sequence is symbolic rather than actual. As though the deer symbolizes the hunted, and her death is the death of all the other animals that are dying all the time: the mice and the voles and the rabbits and the hares.'

Since Rona was highly psychic, she was able to identify with this.

'I am very aware all the time of how close I am to the spiritual, how each tiny gesture or action can take on almost a cosmic significance, and yet, how I do not matter at all. It reminds me of a line from Walt Whitman: "I am large, I contain multitudes". Animals somehow bring us close to the awareness we are born with, that there is far more to everything than just living here as human beings, in the now, thinking our thoughts and reckoning that is all there is to it. I am glad I was that deer. I am glad I died in the same consciousness (or unconsciousness), since she didn't seem to really have much idea of what was going on apart from consciousness of life, and death when it came—as all the other animals have, I am sure. They don't ask questions. They know, without having to be told, the great secrets that we human beings hum and ha about and don't really get anywhere near understanding.'

* * *

Rona's comments underlined the impressions which had come through strongly in other work

178

I had done with animal regressions. In my experience, although all creatures have souls, these are of different types or intensities. When sitters have regressed to life as an animal there is, as I have said, a narrowing of vision into a one-dimensional kind of existence. But in such cases the animal in question has been recognizable as an entity of its own. In my case, for instance, the ginger cat to which I returned was a definite cat, not just 'any' cat. The same feeling comes through when linking with other animal lives.

However, when dealing with creatures such as Gerry's spider, the likelihood would be that it could have been 'any' spider, and so would return at death to a corporate soul. In other cases I have witnessed an animal after death possessing both its own individual soul and a part in the corporate soul of its kind. This is very difficult—almost impossible—to ascertain, but would not affect Gerry's soul having been allowed to 'use' the living body to learn and progress.

Great mystics and visionaries have commented (and will no doubt continue to comment) on the wonder and mystery of animals—so much greater, even though so much less, than ourselves. We can think, to be sure, but, especially when we have experienced what it feels like to exist in animal form, we may wonder whether their blind trust and the devotion that asks no questions and makes no conditions is not something higher than the ability to quibble. Conclusions cannot really be drawn in this field, except that it seems that any soul may incarnate as an animal, and (equally) animals may rise above themselves— progressing, we may take it, in their own spiritual development.

The following lines from Walt Whitman's 'Song of Myself' shed an interesting light on our relationship with our animal 'selves':

> I think I could turn and live with animals, they are so placid and self-contain'd.
> I stand and look at them long and long.
> They do not sweat and whine about their condition.
> They do not lie awake in the dark and weep for their sins.
> They do not make me sick discussing their duty to God.
> Not one is dissatisfied, not one is demented with the mania of owning things.
> Not one kneels to another, nor to his kind that lived thousands of years ago.
> Not one is respectable or unhappy over the whole earth.

CHAPTER TEN

LEGACIES OF THE PAST

Vanessa is regressed and in trance.

She is instructed, 'You reach a door. Go through it and tell me what or who you see.'

She hesitates. Her forehead puckers.

'I can't go through it.' After a pause, she adds, 'I am trying to open it, but it won't open.'

'Okay, it has been opened from the other side. Go through it now.'

More hesitation, then at last she says: 'There's nothing but stones, underfoot. I am falling on stones, and it's dark.'

'Is there anyone else there?'

'I can't see, it's too dark.'

Vanessa's regression took her to a series of visions following the 'dark and stones'. Asked to go forward a few hours, and then days, at a time, she first found herself seemingly on grass. Then she said she was aware of the face of a church clock, square with a pointed dome above, chiming the hour of two. In the next vision, 'I am standing on the grass again, looking at some meat: raw butcher's meat that is cut up and lying in front of me.' The last time she said only, 'The leaves are falling from the trees.'

She seemed unable to relate to anyone and, when asked if other people were there, said there were presences, but she could not understand what they said, if they said anything, and she could not make them out. She also revealed several times that, 'I do not want to be here. I don't feel right. Everything is very confusing. I am very bewildered.'

She thought afterwards that she seemed to have been very small, very confined and restricted, and even said,

'It was as though I was unable to move; I was not aware of the ability to move. I might have been very tightly wrapped up. I did not seem to have had any real shape or form. I was not in pain or frightened, only terribly bewildered. I seemed to be able only to endure—try to keep going in whatever way I could—right from the difficulty in going through the door and the stones tripping me in the dark as I groped and crawled along.'

'That was how you felt, mentally and emotionally, in that life?'

'It seemed more physical really—as though I was a baby that at first did not want to be born, or couldn't be born for some reason. I wondered afterwards if I could have been brain-damaged, and whether I might have been born and then died soon afterwards.'

Following these early visions, and with no break in her regression, she had said that at a time one year, and then two years, later than the falling of the leaves, she was aware of 'Chocolate ... got chocolate on my mouth' (raising an arm to wipe her mouth with the back of her wrist) and of running.

She seemed to have lived an abortive life and then to have been reborn into a more normal existence that (in spite of her efforts to avoid allowing her mind to become influenced) actually seemed to be her present one. She said she had had flashes from early family snapshots at this point. She spoke of 'the room' and 'the box', and said after the session that she knew the room and box (a tin travelling trunk from her childhood) very well—though, when questioned in trance, she did not know the significance of either.

'Perhaps that was it,' she said. 'I was born damaged and came back almost immediately, maybe into the same family. Or else . . . Would it have been possible that I was a twin, and that somehow I was in touch with both the twins, and one died and the other lived?'

The possibilities inherent in this scenario are endless, and cannot now be checked. She could have been born suffering from a serious illness and recovered to live more normally. Or the sensations of dissociation and isolated struggle could have been purely mental.

We carry the past with us into this life, often far more significantly than we know. It is there as an example, to learn from, to give us enlightenment and consolation, and to reassure us that things are indeed proceeding in the proper manner. If there is a problem, it is often helpful just to have some sort of insight into its origins, and, whether we take past-life sessions literally or whether we focus on what they bring to us in association, as it were, their legacy is overwhelming.

Vanessa, for instance, found this particular past life bewildering, confusing and not at all clear, but it gave her encouraging insight into the fact that in this life she has suffered from serious depressive mental illness and emotional isolation.

'How did you feel?' she was asked after the regression.

'Desperately unable to relate or cope, as though it was all wrong. And with no words to explain or any sense that I could do anything— not even cry or scream, which any baby can do. It was just a struggle, without being aware of what it was about. And yet, there were links with life, weren't there? I could see the church clock very clearly, and I knew it was a church clock—and the leaves were falling. I think the butcher's meat was my body, because the "me" who was looking at it was not the "me" who had been doing the struggling; it was the "me" who had come through the door into the stony darkness. She was tall and slender, with long hair, and she seemed to be all in green, with long trailing sleeves. She was fine, no problems, she was real in a sort of strange way. But even the "me" with the chocolate and doing the running, and in "the room" was not her—I was child-size again.'

Vanessa concluded, 'I think I had a tough struggle in some other little body, when I was badly damaged or deformed, and I did not live. But I have carried the bewilderment and confusion and sense of alienation into this life, and it overwhelms me from time to time. My task here is to learn to cope with it; that is why I came back—to try again.'

* * *

Katy went into trance very quickly, but as soon as I suggested she moved backwards in time before birth I could see signs of distress, and her closed eyes brimmed and overflowed with tears. I reassured her.

'It's all right. I want you to turn in through the gate you will see beside you, into a beautiful garden. This garden is peaceful and safe, and you can rest there. It has no connection with anywhere else, and it is very lovely and quiet. There is a pond and fountain, with fish. Can you see them?'

'Yes.' More calmly.

'Is there a bench for you to sit down? Yes, there is. Do you see it?'

'Yes.'

'Then sit down and rest, and while you are here you don't have to worry or try to cope with anything. Tell me what else is in the garden.'

'Goldfish swimming. And tall trees ... shady. No grass.'

'No grass?'

'No, it's all gravel.'

When she was calmer and could proceed, I directed her several times towards paths or gates that would take her to different lives. First, she chose the right-hand path, and when she reached the gate, stopped.

'What is beyond the gate?'

'Nothing. It's like space.'

'Perhaps it is space,' I said and, after a few unproductive, gentle attempts at clarification, brought her back to start again. Her next path took her to:

'The seashore. I'm watching a huge ship— QE2 type of thing—going past.'

She said she seemed to be wearing a sort of swimsuit with a little skirt, but as soon as I began to probe further she became confused and told me that, 'Everything is starting to spin round; all the pictures are going round.'

I brought her back to the garden and then, when she had calmed, tried again. This time she chose another path, but when she reached the gate, stopped without going through it.

'What do you see?' I asked.

'Space, just dark space, like before.'

'Are you waiting for someone?' I enquired.

'No.'

'What do you think would happen if you were to go through the gate?' I asked.

In a small voice she said, 'I think I . . . I think I feel like I could fly.'

'Then fly,' I told her. 'You will be quite safe. Try it and see.'

The tears came oozing from the corners of her eyes again, and in a forlorn murmur, she said,

'If I did, I don't think I would want to come back.'

Then the tears overwhelmed her, and I returned her to the present.

'Well,' I said. 'That explains a lot. You see, you are a Star Child.'

* * *

In her own way, Katy had brought the wisdom and enlightenment from her own past with her, to be revealed in her regression. Star Children are elevated souls who are 'visitors' from a higher plane, with work to do here. They can be recognized in ordinary sittings by their own special 'starry' qualities, and I have mentioned in *A Psychic's Casebook* some of the cases I have encountered. There is generally one overwhelming way in which Star Children can be identified. They have a great longing, which they cannot explain in a rational manner, to 'go home'. However, since they have agreed to accept this life, they cannot return to their own place and their own kind, but their awareness of that other home is something that can reduce them to tears, even though they may not know what they are crying for.

Katy's repeated return, even through different gates, to space—the way home for her—and her intuitive knowledge that she could have 'flown' (but that, if she did so, she would not want to come back) were classic Star Child, according to my experience of Star Children. Also, her emotional response did not seem to be connected with any particular suffering or memories in 'ordinary' human lives in the past. Her real past seemed to be beyond the gates where the space beckoned, her tears those of the spirit in seeming exile and longing to return beyond that space.

Many Star Children are relieved to find there is a reason for their apparently inexplicable feeling that they do not belong on the Earth, that they have a sadness and longing for somewhere they cannot identify. But I have never before come across this being expressed during regression, when the spirit seemed to be trying to leave the Earth for space. It is difficult to know whether Star Children actually experience previous human lives, whether they need to experience them. My feeling is that some—like Katy's seaside vision of the boat— might be planted, as it were, in their consciousness, about as real as a hologram, but giving useful background to substantiate the authenticity of the current 'human' personality.

* * *

Links and legacies from past lives can be found

almost everywhere, even in small ways. The first life I linked into for Bryanne, a well-groomed businesswoman, is recorded in my notes as:

A child dancer, about 7. She travelled around with a 'barn-storming' theatrical company, probably Victorian England. She was dainty, sweet, an inspiration to others, seems to be surrounded by golden light. This was such a happy life. She died young, but was just beautiful while she lived. Her life was a gift to the world.

Bryanne listened to this unmoving, and continued to sit silent while I linked in to several other lives, which were darker, more painful and quite different. At the end, she simply took the paper on which I had scribbled the notes and penned her comments without discussing the matter with me at all. I expected that her comments would concern the heavier, darker lives, but to my amazement, what she wrote was:

First life very interesting, as I have danced for years—all my life!—& the stage and expression within a dance environment is a deep part of my personality. Not sure about the other two.

Sarah, another businesswoman, expressed a

similar type of reaction. The first life I linked in to for her showed me what I described to her as a 'ballet girl': a slip of a creature with luscious, dark hair and eyes, wearing a traditional ballet costume of white tulle and a wreath of flowers on her head. I thought the girl was a dancer at the Paris Opera about 1880. But I did not see her within the theatre; I saw her wearing a cloak over her costume, running across a wide thoroughfare outside it. She was hit by a moving vehicle—some sort of small, fast, horse-drawn cab—and died there on the cobbles, fragile as a lovely, small, white moth in her soft tulle.

'That's all there was,' I said to Sarah. 'She was so beautiful, as though she wasn't human—something light as thistledown and sparkling with life. But she was not intended to live.'

Sarah was fascinated.

'Well, I did learn to dance, and I always felt I should be a dancer. Not just a young girl's passing dream, you know, something much deeper. I always felt there was something there, something to do with dancing.'

* * *

Often the past brings with it a legacy of hard-earned personal wisdom and instruction for living this life. So many examples of this, which occur time after time when conducting past-life sittings and regressions, cannot possibly be

190

mere coincidence. No one has ever accused me personally of inventing the visions which emerge, but I have examined the possibility myself. I reached the conclusion long since that, if, within the few moments when I take the hands of complete strangers, link to them and provide them with 'lives' of such significance and import (and with which, more often than not, they are able to identify emotionally), my mind could weigh up their needs without some sort of higher power and vision to guide me, then I would be one of the greatest geniuses ever born. I prefer to believe that I am given the visions I see and the ability to put them to positive use.

* * *

Alice, a psychic artist of incredible mental detachment, sat down with me for a past-life session. The notes I made about her 'lives' ran as follows:

First Life: A composed young woman, late Victorian era, about 15, somewhere in the Midlands or North of England. She was the daughter of a professional man (mother seems absent—probably dead). She was extremely adult in her ways, very aware of the brain and its potential—mixed with older people a lot, developed her own ideas. She decided to devote herself to solving a problem concerning water/drainage/crop irrigation in India (obviously thought on 'Empire' lines) and went there. She lived a busy, masculine sort of life, no emotional ties; worked hard, died in India of wound in the side, buried there.

Second Life: Further back chronologically, but difficult to date. Chinaman, very small; developed fireworks, particularly with regard to wide, far-flung explosions of colour. No close relationships.

Third Life: About 1300. At first I see a large, gentle lay-brother in a monastery—gardener. Loved the flowers and made their cultivation his whole existence. He just lived moment by moment and *felt*.

At the same time I also pick up what seems like an *alter ego* (the Abbot?—or, at any rate, a superior to the lay-brother): sharp, quick brain—impatient, angry. Wants the other removed.

The message I received for Alice from these lives was that she should try to resolve the conflict that seemed to have developed in her past between the coolness of thought and the richness of sensation. Her brain and her emotional responses had become detached from each other; it appeared that the conflict had resulted in an increasing detachment—which I felt strongly even in the present. She found all her answers in brain-power and could not, like the lay-brother, appreciate the joy of

192

simply *being*. I added, 'Do not anticipate the wider picture. Let rational and logical thought go, and simply *be*.'

* * *

Robina has previously consulted me about her difficult personal relationship, and we have established that, though successful at work and in the competitive world, she is sadly lacking in confidence and self-respect. She is inclined to be destructive in her relationship, simply because she cannot believe she is worthy of love, and so distrusts it when it is offered.

Things are improving, but she is interested now in the spiritual side, and has requested a past-life session. I link in with her first life.

'This has come very quickly. I see your hands, reaching out and up, twining together. They are covered with blood, and I think you are reaching up to a small gap in the wall above your head. You were shut in an institution of some kind, but I am not sure whether it was an asylum or a prison. There were people all around, a noise that never stopped—shouting and screaming, crying—bodies moving all the time, and you do not want to acknowledge them. I do not know why you have been shut in, and you don't seem to have known yourself; I think you were not very old, and you have landed up there by chance or accident. You have been reaching for that little gap all the time. Your hands are raw with scraping at the stone walls—big, rough stones—in an attempt to get out.'

'And yet,' I say thoughtfully. 'There is something not quite right here. You could not actually get through the gap at all. It is more of a compulsive act, this movement of the hands—as though you are doing what you can to distance yourself from what is around you. And it is done with such passion that your bleeding hands seem far more real to me than the scene at the back of you, where the rest of the people are.'

When Robina applies this to her life in the present, she comments,

'It is a bit the same, isn't it? Not being able to accept the realities of my situation—that I need to trust in the love I am offered and feel free to love in return. We've mentioned realities before; they can change so, and often the threats that seem so frightening to me just aren't there. I seem to be like . . . trying to get away from a reality that frightened me but pushing myself into a dead end, hurting myself.'

'More than the actual reality in the past life was hurting, seemingly because you were all right except for the noise and the presence of a lot of people,' I point out.

As we concentrate on the situation, the picture clears a little further.

'Somewhere—whether further along the

194

wall or not, I don't know—there is a big floor-to-ceiling door (more like a double door really, like a complete wall of bars). And people are passing by on the other side, not prison officers or staff or attendants, but ordinary people in quite elaborate clothes. I have only a vague image: something like tall hats, tight trousers, voluminous shawls. You did not see them clearly, or, if you did, their clothes did not register much. But here we have a third reality. They were real, standing outside the bars watching the scene inside. You tried to reach them too, but it was like reaching out your hands to figures in a dream. Which was really real? This is your problem, isn't it? Something for you to think about.'

'Did I ever get out?' she asks hopefully.

'I cannot tell that. Probably not. But the real way through would have been to accept the reality you had been forced into, make it your own and make the best of it, taking what positivity you could from the situation. Easier said than done,' I comment.

Her second life comes smashing through, just as vividly as the first, and just as narrow in its vision. I see first a blazing red cross on a white background, the surcoat of a man sitting astride a horse, and I tell her:

'Well, this is one of the few times I can say I see a real person, someone I can recognize historically. I am seeing King Richard I of England—the Lionheart—and I thought at first you were his wife, but you are not. You are of much lower social standing, some type of serving woman, I think. You are young and in the entourage, or whatever they called it, as he travelled round during the Crusades. The point is, though, that you saw him—as I am seeing him now, on his horse—and you simply loved him heart and soul, with all your being. You would have died for him.'

'Really?' she says faintly.

'Yes. But again the realities are rearing their ugly heads. You worshipped, this time unreservedly, giving him what you would have given a god. To you he was perfect. This is true "unreserved love and trust": the attitude we have to aim at in our relationships. But there was another reality you were unaware of. This man was a homosexual, he would not have looked at any woman twice. To him, you and your adoration might well not have been there at all.'

'That is interesting,' she says.

It seems as though Robina's past lives are providing her with different patterns that add up to the same truth, that the question of realities—so complex and tangled and, in her case, so difficult to cope with in her personal relationships—is being spelled out for her and illustrated. I feel that her lives were largely static, wasted in dead-end beating against circumstances, or in proffering or entering into an emotional state that cannot materialize

196

further because its full reality is not appreciated. Also, her lives seem to have been out of her own control, waiting all the time on events regulated by others.

We try a third life.

After a pause, I say: 'This is amazing. But I will give it to you as I get it. I see and feel a boat, gently rocking on placid water, at night, the sky is dark overhead. You are lying down—or sideways—against the front of the boat, and you are a child, I think, but I am not sure what sex. There are a lot of other people sleeping in the boat as well, wrapped in their heavy robes.

'This is the Sea of Galilee, and only a short distance from you, across the slanting seats, is the man we know as Christ, wrapped up like the others and sleeping. You could reach out and touch him, almost. But the interesting thing is that you do not like him—or, more accurately, you feel threatened by him. You wish he was not there, or that he would go away.

'You really have lived in elevated company in the past.'

Robina is listening in fascination.

'One more set of realities, isn't it? You lived through the events of Christ's ministry—or some of them, at any rate—as a child and knew him well. But, though you recognized his divinity . . . his power, call it what you will . . . it represented not new life to you, excitement and hope, but trouble brewing. You knew he made things happen—and you resented his presence,

197

because you wanted things to stay the way they were. I feel you might have been a young relative of one of the fishermen, and you just got swept along with the crowds, as it were. The others believed and participated in what was happening; you stood aloof. The same way you did in the other lives, really. You do not ever seem to have lived, even though you were present at some supreme moments in history. You just looked on—and, more importantly, chose the most negative ways of regarding the situation. One has to be prepared to take a risk, not wait for a cast-iron guarantee that everything will be all right. Your message here, very clearly, is that life does not work that way. There is no such thing as all right; you must make the best of what you are given, make your choices and be positive about them. The same realities can mean quite different things to different people—life to one, death to another. The choice is entirely yours.'

CHAPTER ELEVEN

DEVIL'S ADVOCATE: THE CASE AGAINST

If the past lives that can be remembered, realized or contacted via the methods detailed in this book are not genuine (as sceptics assert) and do not mean we have lived before, then what are they? Do past lives exist at all—or do we live only in the present life, the present moment, the *now*? Is everything else, even our memory of other time, nothing but a dream?

It is only fair to examine this question seriously. For it is a fact that there are all kinds of explanations that could account for the phenomena we call past lives. There can be physical, chemical or mental accounting for almost every detail of past-life and related activity.

So what are these explanations? The most obvious is that both the person who claims to remember a past life or lives and the practitioner (such as myself) who contacts them on behalf of sitters are not telling the truth, whether deliberately or for some deeply unconscious reason.

As a clairvoyant, psychic and mystic, my belief is that telepathy is the only really honest method of communication. All forms of language can actually be used to *prevent* the truth from being perceived by others, and words may actually be expressing the opposite of what they seem to be saying. There are many unhappy people who, like difficult children seeking attention, cannot state the truth and instead invent stories of all kinds that have no validity in them at all. If they think their friends would be impressed, why not reveal their own 'past life' as Charles II or Nell Gwynne, Cleopatra, Julius Caesar or Lucrezia Borgia?

There are others who do not intend to deceive but whose perceptions are not clear, their judgement flawed. They might have read or heard something in the past and forgotten it. When it swims back up to their conscious mind (and the mind is capable of the most amazing tricks) the experience is so vivid that they identify with it and feel they know it so well it have happened to them. This is almost impossible to verify, because it is done in all innocence with no conscious fakery, and is believed in absolutely by the person concerned.

It is not generally realized just how one's conscious and unconscious awareness can confuse and deceive. Nor is it realized how much information the averagely-educated child can absorb and retain during its formative years—often, as it were, by a type of osmosis. I can now recollect being present as a very young child in the room where a pregnant woman was about to give birth. Much later, as a teenager, I can also recall reading the pathetic details of a birth scene witnessed surreptitiously (it was, if I am not wrong, in Alexander Cordell's historical novel *The Rape of the Fair Country*). Out of a confusion of these two things, snatches of conversation and other memories I could easily have deluded myself that I had been present at such a scene and witnessed this painful birth (or even given birth as a poor Welsh woman myself in secret and dreadful trauma), though in fact I have never done so.

As another example, I might claim I had known a past life as a hunter on the plains of North America, about a hundred or so years ago, and describe in revolting detail the traditional methods of killing and skinning animals—a subject I know nothing about and the thought of which turns my stomach. This would be a genuine case of 'How could I possibly know all this awful stuff unless I had actually been there and lived like that?' Yet, on reflection (if I reflected long enough), I might remember that I had once, aged perhaps twelve, read at least one novel that contained such details, including the classic *The Deer Slayer* by James Fenimore Cooper. Lives in ancient Rome can easily take form and detail from books in most libraries—*Quo Vadis?*, *The Last Days of Pompeii*, *The Robe*—and any number of educational books, magazines and television programmes. This applies also to other favourite periods of history.

And what about the practitioner who 'sees' your past lives for you? Why might he or she lie? Regrettably, the urge for power, for manipulation, for reputation, is as great now as it has ever been, and it seems probable (though it cannot be proved) that at any rate some practitioners make a little vision go a long way, to say the least. Wherever human beings are concerned, the truth has to be in question all the time.

Even without meaning to do so, a hypnotist

can influence the sitter—through the way questions are phrased, even by the tone of voice—so that the sitter may find ideas planted in his head, deliberately or not. In my experience, this is most likely to happen when genuine past-life personae are vague and unhelpful, and there does not seem to be much to offer the sitter. But these dazed and bewildered, barely articulate voices are more than likely to be those of the most genuine cases, and the glib, all-questions-answered, everything-accounted-for types should be regarded with suspicion.

It is also important that evidence from past-life sittings should be accurately recorded and adhered to afterwards. The flattering interest of family and friends can change accounts of what was really said and felt at the time into glamourized versions that sound so much more impressive. Conclusions are also inclined to be drawn afterwards which may not actually fit the evidence that was given. The human mind has a great capacity for tidying up loose ends and making things fit conveniently. A square peg of past-life session is often, even before the sitter has left the sitting, on the way to being shaped to fit the round hole that seems so much more satisfactory to everyone.

One possibility that should be considered is that the recollections, the memories and experiences that seem to occur as fragments of past life may be entirely composed of hallucinations or delusions of some form or another. Mental illness can bring the subject of past lives very frighteningly close to home— although schizophrenics, for instance, follow a pattern that is quite different to the patterns of lives revealed in 'past-life sittings'.

Celine, a nurse I tutored for a Postal Course in writing, revealed in her first communications that she wanted to write her life story. It was so amazing, she said, and so many incredible things had happened to her. A little further on I was hearing what some of those incredible happenings were. She had discovered that she was the 'reincarnation' of Hitler, and that she and her family (there were not enough brothers and sisters, so some cousins had been included as well) had lived before as the Twelve Disciples of Christ. Celine herself had been Judas, and she revealed matter-of-factly that it was because of the sins committed in her earlier lives as Judas and Hitler, that she was being punished now.

Even before she actually allowed me to know that she was a diagnosed schizophrenic, I was well aware of the fact, and, whether or not she had indeed lived previous lives, I was sure she had not been Hitler or Judas. Paranoia arising from mental illness and the inability to relate to reality—imagining, for instance, that the voices in the television set are talking about you and know everything you are doing—has no part in the spiritual enlightenment and positivity to be gained by becoming aware of the past and using it wisely to build a better future. Genuine past-life cases indicate the involvement of each soul with the natural progression and order of things—the relative insignificance of the individual, as well as the fact that no single living thing is ever forgotten. Mental illness, on the whole, focuses on the individual, even if this focus takes the form of self-punishment or self-abasement.

Then there are experiences of so-called *déjà vu*, which convince many people that 'I have been here before'. *Déjà vu* can in fact be explained in purely physical terms. It is caused when one part of the brain (the right or left hemisphere) works independently of the other hemisphere; perception of reality is thus flawed, as one side of the brain works a fraction quicker than the other. This creates a fractional time difference in perception that gives the sensation of 'previous experience' of a place or situation, of feeling one has gone through a particular time-span before. This can happen at any time to anyone. It is clinically known as 'double arousal' and is prompted by deep emotion, such as awe or wonderment. There does not appear to be any psychic or supernatural reason for it.

However, although this phenomenon might promote a sense of strange familiarity (a sense of saying words that were said before, or of performing actions already carried out at some unspecified, earlier time), it is worth considering whether it could account, for instance, for someone in a place that they have never in their life visited before having a detailed awareness *before they turn a corner* of the view to be seen once they have turned it. The view might have been seen in a painting, on a postcard, or in some other weird and wonderful coincidental manner—as a wallpaper design, on a fabric, or from a plane, even—but there are other instances of *déjà vu* that cannot be so conveniently dismissed. How, for instance, could anyone possibly possess intimate and accurate knowledge of the existence of papers, maps, documents—or of the former state of buildings demolished or renovated centuries ago—that no other single person in the world is aware of? Such cases happen, and are generally regarded as flights of fancy—until, unexpectedly, verification in the form of archaeological finds (or even investigations suggested by the person himself) comes to light.

Perhaps the most common and widest-ranging explanation that can be given for delusions of past living is the influence of drugs. Hallucinatory drugs can cause hallucinations ('trips'), delusions of omnipotence and all-encompassing awareness. Mescalin-based drugs have in fact been used time out of mind to help achieve altered states of consciousness and higher realities. They are used in shamanistic training of the mind through fantasies and visions, not only of beauty but also of horror, suffering and confusion, on the path to enlightenment and wisdom.

No one can deny that altered states of mind and altered realities can occur as a result of the use of drugs or other agents—whether alcohol, LSD, opium, or even therapeutically prescribed medication, such as lithium carbonate or diazepam. So can altered consciousness of individual power and potential. Maybe the fantasy worlds of the drugged—even the mañana attitude, which, in reality, means 'tomorrow will never actually come'—have significance and validity, but do they shed any light on past lives? Few people actually claim to have experienced their regressive memories while under the influence of drugs; most are only too obviously in the 'normal' state of tension and stress that marks our living today. The tiny percentage who may 'dream' a past life that will hold water while actually in a drugged state is not a very convincing argument for attributing all experience of past lives to substance abuse.

It was Carl Jung who coined the term 'Collective Unconscious'. But, long before the revelations of psychiatry, ancient spiritual leaders had always known there was a race memory, a 'stream of consciousness' and of awareness of life that the soul could (when the time was right) dip into and refresh itself, re-assert its own existence and touch again the divine spring from which it had come. From those who have passed before, from the legacy of human caring and compassion, those who are still struggling may receive guidance and encouragement, as well as, however intuitively, knowledge to assist them in the process of day-to-day existence.

Many of the things we pick up around us that seem to be outside the scope of our conscious awareness or our human senses do probably arise from the race memories latent within. Belief that a fire is comforting as well as warming stems, no doubt, from an atavistic recollection of long nights when hungry beasts were only kept at bay by the circle of firelight within which we crouched. Unease when a thunderstorm fizzles and crashes overhead probably owes its existence to a centuries-old awareness of what damage the storm could do—whether by means of magic or electricity—if it should strike.

Many things may come from the Collective Unconscious which flesh out recollections of past lives: behavioural traits, for instance, or social habits of the past, even sometimes details of what it has been like to have lived before. And because so many people lived lives that, in their way, might have been regarded as almost identical (the role of slaves, peasants, natives or tribesmen, even women, in many civilizations hardly varied from century to century), it might even seem that two people could be linking up to the same life.

But this is where, for me, the case for past lives really comes into its own—and it is something that can only be appreciated and accepted on a spiritual level. I have found, as I have detailed in this book, that no two lives were exactly the same. Each was occupied by a separate soul, something unique that was feeling its way, however fumblingly, towards the end of that stretch of its road.

The miracle of dealing with past lives, for me, is not what people remember nor what I, as their link and channel, can reveal for them. It is in the fact that at each session, out of literally millions upon millions of potential lives, the sitters are unerringly directed to the one, or two, or three which are intensely personal to them. It is as though they have been able to turn back the pages in the Recording Angel's book and read an account of their soul's progress so far, what has been achieved, and what is still to learn.

How far have I got? What have I learned so far? What is there still to do? And how much further to go? These are the questions that can be answered—whether in images or in symbols, in information that can be put to use today or in explanations that help to clarify emotional problems of a lifetime's standing, in visions of karmic debts to be paid or in approval for bitter struggles that have earned their bright reward. In whatever language our past lives speak to us, they do so individually and privately, with far more relevance than any generalization could do. Whatever might have happened in the past, it did not happen to holograms and cardboard cut-outs. We—in some shape or form—were all there. And now we are a little further along the road, that is all.

CHAPTER TWELVE

PAST LIFE MEMORY: A BRIEF GUIDE TO EXPLORING YOUR OWN PAST LIVES

There is no reason why anyone cannot have at least some success in exploring and investigating their own past lives. The following basic points need to be understood first of all:

1. If you do not seriously believe reincarnation is possible and treat the subject as a joke, you will not progress very far.
2. Even if you do take the matter seriously, you will need to spend more than the odd half-hour working on your regressions. As with all spiritual and psychic work, a great deal of self-discipline is involved, as well as mental awareness and a willingness to submit to

developing your higher powers. You will need to make your sessions part of your everyday life and to work on what you are doing maybe once a week—at least to start off with.

3. Releasing the traumas of your past lives can be painful as well as beneficial, as we have seen. Work with a companion, so that if anything becomes difficult you have a supportive presence at hand. Remember that the results of any form of regression can continue to develop long after you have actually stopped thinking about it with your conscious mind. Be aware of changes within yourself and understand the reason for them.

4. Keep notes of whatever occurs as a result of your investigations. Even if you cannot understand what it means, be scrupulously accurate, and do not try to draw conclusions until you have some experience with the 'feel' of past-life existence. Remember that you may experience personae unlike any within your present awareness and, even if things seem strange or odd, keep exactly to the facts as you perceive them; do not try to make anything 'fit'. Do not forget to include details that might seem insignificant or even meaningless, and keep a complete record.

Session Techniques

After I wrote *A Psychic's Casebook* many people asked for instructions on how to

210

develop their psychic potential. Basically, any spiritual or psychic work—including, of course, work with your past lives—requires the disciplines of *Relaxation, Concentration* and *Visualization*. These will not only free your mind and potential but also help enormously in your everyday life and lessen tension and stress, making you far more aware of the real richness of living—which is an added bonus.

You may start a session with *Relaxation*, and some exercises to help you concentrate. Follow with a specific exercise for past-life memory. Work out your needs to suit yourself, but do remember that there is no short cut through the difficult bits. If you cannot relax, do not tell yourself it doesn't matter; it does. The ability to be still and calm, without as well as within, is the foundation on which all the rest of the work is done. So persevere.

The Session

You (and your companion) need a quiet place where you can relax and will not be disturbed for half an hour or so. You may prefer to lie flat on your back, or to sit in an upright chair. Try both, and see which suits you best. Make sure you do not get cold, and have a light blanket ready if necessary. Be careful that you do not fall asleep during the relaxation—the aim is to relax but to keep the mind alert.

Have pen and paper to hand, and a soothing

tape of natural sound—the sea, water flowing, a fountain, bird songs—to play while you sit or lie comfortably.

Basic Relaxation Technique

Relaxation is achieved by two means: controlled breathing and letting go of tension in the body.

First concentrate on your breathing, becoming more and more aware of the breath passing in and out of your nostrils. Try to breathe in to a count of three, then hold your breath for a count of three, and then exhale to a count of three. When you feel comfortable doing this, you can move on to a count of four, and later five, as you breathe in and out.

Count as you breathe for a few breaths only—say ten. Then breathe normally. Next (if you are in a prone position) place your hands lightly on your abdomen, so that the tips of your fingers touch across the navel. Try a deep breath, drawing the air right to the bottom of your lungs so that your abdomen rises and lifts your hands; then breathe out and let your hands fall. Attempt this only four times per session. Then return to normal breathing.

Following your breathing exercises, you will work at relaxing the muscle groups in the body.

Begin with your toes and feet. Tighten the muscles of your toes, screw them up, hold for a moment, then relax. Then do the same with the

212

muscles of your ankles. Hold tightly then relax. Follow the same procedure with all your muscle groups in turn—calves and knees; thighs; hips; abdomen; hands; arms; shoulders; chest; neck and head—and finally clench your jaw, screw up your face and eyes, then relax.

By this time, if you are not accustomed to regular relaxation, you will find when you go back to your toes, that they are now tense. Try the whole series of exercises over again.

For the moment, it is enough to discipline yourself into actually taking time to work on each group of muscles. Do not worry if they quickly become tense once more. It takes time to learn relaxation, and no effort you spend on it will be lost.

Basic Concentration Technique

Having gone through your breathing and relaxation technique, turn to Concentration.

Make sure you are comfortable, warm and not sleepy. Close your eyes and examine what you can 'see' within your mind. Darkness? Colours? Images? Shapes? It does not matter where you think these colours or shapes come from, whether from your actual eyes or from your imagination. Simply examine them, note what you see then put it aside.

Now open your eyes and focus your attention on something in the room. You may like to provide an uplifting object (a flower, a

213

gemstone, a coloured candle, for instance) beforehand. Look steadily at this object and concentrate on it. Try to absorb it into your mind, to enter into it and let it enter into you. Do not analyse it, simply accept it for what it is.

The aim in this exercise is not to 'look at' the object and then look away, nor to try to memorize what it looks like. If you can concentrate, quietly and fully, for some time on a lovely object like a rose or a piece of quartz crystal, you will find that your 'look' has become a two-way affair, and a silent, beautiful dialogue is now taking place.

Spiritual wisdom is attained not by 'doing' but by 'being'—and concentration is the study of the ability to 'be' in harmony and peacefulness. As a final exercise before you start working with the past, imagine you are standing underneath a waterfall of beautiful clear water, lifting your face to it. The water is washing the worries and cares of the present away, leaving you fresh and ready to begin your journey into the past. Let the water cleanse you and purge you.

When finishing your relaxation exercises, take a deep breath, have a good stretch and take your time before you rise or move from the floor or chair, moving slowly.

Basic Past Life Technique

Now switch on your tape and lie (or sit)

relaxed, breathing deeply, detaching your mind from everything in the present and linking in with the everlasting ebb and flow of the cycles of life. While you spend about five minutes letting the sounds lift you above the everyday pressures of existence, ponder on the following directive. If convenient, it may be read aloud, or it can be taped and played as part of the session.

If only I take the trouble consciously to let go of the present—safely, here in this quiet place that will hold me until I return to pick up my life in the present again—it is easy to let my spirit drift, like a white feather on a soft wind, or a flower petal on the sea's gentle waves. I am a part of nature; I am one with the snow and the sunlight and the fiery stars, the seams of dark rock beneath the place where my feet have walked.

A great river of life flows eternally, and I am a part of that river. I will step carefully into the water with my bare feet, let go of the reeds at the bank, and let the water take me where it will. At any time, I can return to this quiet place in safety. My spirit is drifting, drifting . . .

Allow a few moments of concentration, with eyes shut, imagining that you are taking a few steps down the river. Then, when you feel you wish to leave the water, imagine yourself setting your foot on the first of a flight of shallow steps, holding safely onto the rail at the side, and climbing out of the water.

Spend a few minutes simply visualizing yourself at the top of the steps, in your new surroundings. Then take up your pen and paper, including a list of questions that you have previously prepared. If you are on your own, write down the answers as accurately and fully as possible. If you are with a companion, they may ask you the questions in a quiet, detached manner and may also include further questions about the facts and details you are giving them in your answers. Keep this as matter-of-fact as possible.

List of Questions to Guide Past Life Memory

1. Describe the place where you are standing. (Outdoors? Indoors? Trees? Houses? Seashore? Fields? Woodland?)
2. Starting from your feet and moving upwards, concentrate on what you are wearing. (Shoes or barefoot? What sort of clothes? Fabrics? Do they fit? Patterns and colours? Do you like or dislike them? Your hair—is it styled or loose? Long or short? Anything you can add about what you wear in your hair, or the way it has been done?
3. Are you aware of whether you are male or female?
4. Are you aware (roughly) of your age?

216

5. How does your body feel? (Fit and healthy? Tired and aching? Weak? Ill?)
6. Concentrate on what you are doing in the place where you have found yourself. Are you content to be there or unhappy?
7. Are you alone? If not, can you describe who is with you and their relationship to you? What are they doing? Do you like or dislike them?
8. Do you have a name? If so, can you give it?
9. What is your favourite food? And drink? Game or sport? Relaxation?
10. Any further details to have emerged from the session.

When you are ready, return to the handrail and the steps down into the water. Imagine yourself walking down them and wading a few yards upstream. Allow yourself to let go of everything you have just experienced, to wash it away in the healing waters of the river. The past will always be there whenever you wish to return to it, but it is time past and does not belong in the present. Envisage the quiet place waiting for you, and feel yourself return safely and peacefully to your own body and personality in the present.

*   *   *

Second Past Life Session
Relax in the way already described, with natural sounds, and with eyes shut allow

yourself to drift backwards through your past, reminding yourself that you are safe, relaxing, and can return safely at any time. If any doubt is felt about this, make sure you are with a companion who will instruct you to return and, once you have done so, will remind you that you are safely back in the present.

The exercises described here do not involve hypnosis, and there should normally be no difficulty with 'past-life memory'. What you are actually doing is helping yourself to remember, in the same way that you might try to remember events that happened when you were a child. For most people many memories of this sort will already have surfaced in the form of dreams or spontaneous recollections which might have been difficult to explain, or which you put down to imagination.

Your past-life memory is like a muscle—one that does not work easily, because it does not have much exercise. These basic visualizations and exercises enable you to start using your muscle, though you must not expect to achieve wonderful results immediately. As with anything else that involves skilled usage, practise will be necessary.

While drifting in your second exercise, tell yourself you are returning to a self that you knew in the past. This self is at present sleeping, and, when you make contact, your presence will be the signal for it to wake and the day to begin. Visualize yourself waking up

218

as that other self, perhaps stretching and, without stopping to think about it, hurrying to dress.

Perhaps there is furniture in the room where you find yourself, or perhaps there may not be—you may be sleeping somewhere where furniture would not belong.

However, tell yourself that you have brought with you a long mirror—a cheval glass on a stand. This is so that you can see what you look like. At some stage, take a look in the mirror to examine yourself and what you are wearing.

Have paper and pen ready, and write down what you see. Also make a rough sketch of what you see in the mirror and any other points of interest.

If, as this past self, you have other clothes, imagine you have brought a large wardrobe or chest with you to store them. Visualize yourself trying to decide what to wear for a special day, and trying on the contents of the wardrobe or chest.

When you feel ready, tell yourself that it is the end of the day, and time to sleep. Let your past self prepare for the night, perhaps putting on night attire after undressing. Make notes of anything worn at night and try to catch a glimpse of it in your mirror.

When your past self is peacefully sleeping, allow the past to rest and return to your present body and personality (mentally bringing your mirror and wardrobe with you!).

* * *

Early sessions with past-life memory will probably not need to be longer than twenty minutes or half an hour. You may find vizualisation difficult at first, as we have seen, and some people will find they are real beginners at the art of concentrating. This is not surprising, because concentration is something that is not encouraged in modern living (the attention span of the average television viewer, for instance, is only a few minutes, while makers of advertisements know that they need to get their message across in a matter of seconds). But relaxation, the ability to be aware of the power of the mind, the reality of thought and the visions that will come if the way is clear for them, are all part of the learning process when dealing with past lives.

In early sessions you may find you feel frustrated, because there seems to be no result, and just give up; or else you may become excited, if you get through to a 'life' that seems detailed and vivid, and feel tempted to keep on indefinitely. In either case, keep to your intended time, then close the session as though you have just finished a session of relaxation, giving yourself a good stretch and 'switching off' all connections with the past.

After Each Session

Do not examine the notes or sketches you have made immediately. Wait until a little time has elapsed—and, even then, remember to take everything at its face value and not try to read in details that were not present. I personally always find that, because of my calling as a psychic and mystic, I hardly ever notice things like the colour of men's or women's skin, or their hair—not because of any prejudice or lack of it, but because I link up with their souls and 'miss' bodily details.

If you are new to past lives, however, it is very important that you develop your memory by means of such small details. The head-dresses of the men in white robes that I mentioned in connection with Angie's case—and which I sketched because I could not describe them very well—might well have turned out later to belong to the 'Incas' who were described by another psychic as 'surrounding' her. But I did not identify them as Inca, nor did I feel that the men themselves had Inca 'energy' about them.

When working with past lives, it is vital that you begin to get a feel for the truth, and that you do not allow yourself to be influenced away from exactly what you saw, felt and experienced—even if your impressions were vague, or if it seems as though you must have been wrong.

The most important skill you can acquire when working in this field is the ability to trust the pictures and impressions of the past that you are given. Most people find it very difficult to 'take' the open channel down which the memories flow, and they allow their brains to get in the way, beginning to question and examine—and doubt.

You will find such sessions are far less melodramatic than the popular idea of a regression session to past lives, with the sitter prone on a couch while a hypnotist swings a glittering object in front of his eyes and mutters: 'Back . . . back . . . you are returning to the past . . . going back in time . . .'. At this stage, my opinion is that regression under hypnosis—or even self-hypnosis—should only be attempted under skilled supervision. For the moment, your 'past-life memory', if properly used, can work for you every bit as well.

SELECTED READING

Bernstein, Morey, *The Search for Bridey Murphy* (Pocket Books, New York, 1978)

Dunne, J.W., *An Experiment with Time* rev. edn, introduction by Brian Inglis (Macmillan, 1981)

Fisher, Joe, *The Case for Reincarnation* (Collins, 1984)

Gater, Dilys, *A Psychic's Casebook* (Robert Hale, 1995)

Grant, Joan, *Winged* (Sphere, 1973)

—— *Life as Carola* (Sphere, 1973)

—— *Far Memory* (Corgi, 1975)

Grey, Margot, *Return from Death* (Arkana, 1985)

Moody, Dr Raymond A., jr., *Life after Life* (Bantam Books, 1981)

Moss, Peter, with Keaton, Joe, *Encounters with the Past* (Penguin, 1981)

Evans-Wentz, W.Y. (ed), *The Tibetan Book of the Dead* (Oxford, 1960)

Sambhava, Padma, *The Tibetan Book of the Dead*, trans Robert A.F. Thurman— (Aquarian/Thorsons, 1994)

Verney, Dr Thomas with Kelly, John, *The Secret Life of the Unborn Child* (Sphere 1981)

Zukav, Gary, *The Dancing Wu Li Masters - An Overview of the New Physics* (Bantam Books, 1980)

We hope you have enjoyed this Large Print book. Other Chivers Press or Thorndike Press Large Print books are available at your library or directly from the publishers.

For more information about current and forthcoming titles, please call or write, without obligation, to:

Chivers Press Limited
Windsor Bridge Road
Bath BA2 3AX
England
Tel. (01225) 335336

OR

Thorndike Press
P.O. Box 159
Thorndike, Maine 04986
USA
Tel. (800) 223-2336

All our Large Print titles are designed for easy reading, and all our books are made to last.